MINOR ASPECTS BETWEEN NATAL PLANETS

Books by Emma Belle Donath

Approximate Positions of Asteroids, 1851-2050
Asteroids in the Birth Chart, revised
Asteroids in Midpoints, Aspects and Planetary Pictures
Asteroids in Synastry
Asteroids in the U.S.A. (asteroid research)
Have We Met Before?
Houses: Which and When
Minor Aspects Between Natal Planets
Patterns of Professions
Planetary Declinations: North & South (forthcoming)
Relocation

MINOR ASPECTS

BETWEEN NATAL PLANETS

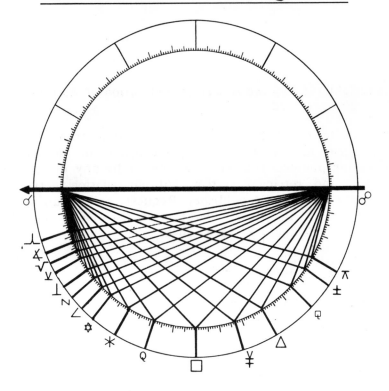

Emma Belle Donath

Published By

American Federation Of Astrologers

First Printing 1981
Fifth Printing 1990
ISBN Number: 0-86690-013-6
Library of Congress Number: 81-69738

Published by:
American Federation of Astrologers, Inc.
P.O. Box 22040, 6535 South Rural Road
Tempe, Arizona 85285-2040

Printed in the United States of America

"And He saw a certain poor widow casting in thither two mites...She of her want did cast in all the living she had...and it was valued as highly as the many talents of the wealthy."
Luke XXI: 1-4
Holy Bible, RSV

TABLE OF CONTENTS

Preface

Much of the information in this book was obtained through research done several years ago in preparing an article for Stellium Quarterly magazine which is edited and published by Kt Boehrer from El Paso, Texas. At that time I was intrigued by comments made in the best-seller *Passages,* by Gail Sheehy. She seemed to be proving astrological timing without mentioning planets, houses or signs. A rather lengthy article, entitled Astrology Answers Passages, was prepared and printed in two issues of Stellium Quarterly. Since then numerous persons have requested copies of that article and further information on the work with minor aspects between planets. This book is being written in answer to those requests. The article is reprinted, with permission of Mrs. Boehrer, as the chapter on Cycles of Aspects.

Because of the continuing controversy over use of Tropical Signs or Sidereal Constellations I have omitted all reference to signs, houses or personal points in the delineations of minor aspects. Therefore, the geometric distance between actual planets is the only thing considered in this book.

Emma Belle Donath

Dayton, Ohio
January, 1981

Cycles of Aspects

By astrologically charting the various ages it becomes apparent that not only are major planetary cycles and aspects significant but so-called minor aspects are also. All events and ages can be divided into Marker Events and Developmental Phases, to coin two phrases from the book *Passages,* by Gail Sheehy. Marker Events describe concrete happenings which the world can see. Developmental Phases are periods where changes begin within the individual to become outer changes or not. As man is said to respond to septenary influences, the charts for each seven years of life are presented and catalogued according to Marker or Developmental in Figure 1.

Marker Events and Developmental Phases
Figure 1

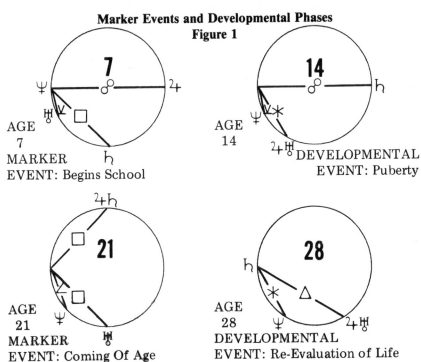

AGE 7
MARKER EVENT: Begins School

AGE 14
DEVELOPMENTAL EVENT: Puberty

AGE 21
MARKER EVENT: Coming Of Age

AGE 28
DEVELOPMENTAL EVENT: Re-Evaluation of Life

Figure 1 (Cont.)

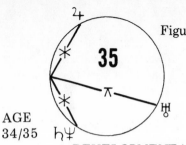

AGE
34/35
DEVELOPMENTAL
EVENT: Seeds Planted For
Insight

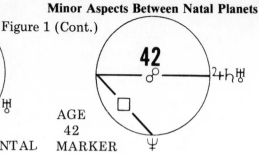

AGE
42
MARKER
EVENT: Changes In Life Style

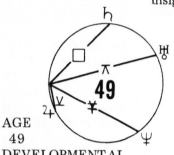

AGE
49
DEVELOPMENTAL
EVENT:Menopause

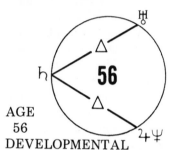

AGE
56
DEVELOPMENTAL
EVENT: Prepare For Job
Retirement

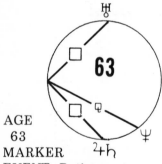

AGE
63
MARKER
EVENT: Retirement

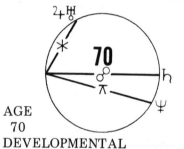

AGE
70
DEVELOPMENTAL
PHASE: Decreasing of Physical
Energies

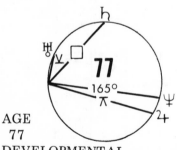

AGE
77
DEVELOPMENTAL
EVENT: Mental Withdrawl

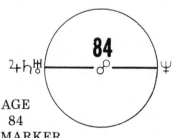

AGE
84
MARKER
EVENT: Transit To New Cycle

Because of retrogradation, positions of natal planets and other astronomical factors, the ages at which various cycles will affect the individual are determined by the precise birth chart. A variation of two or three years from the information discussed is normal.

Further, in *Passages,* the individual is considered to have two basic portions of the personality — the Merger Self and the Seeker Self. Astrological-

Birth to Puberty

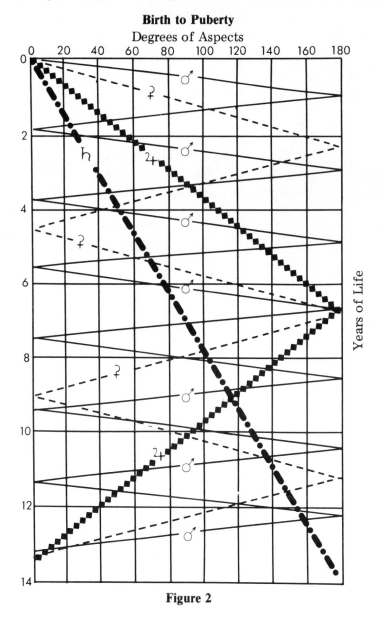

Figure 2

3

ly, the Merger Self would compare with Saturn, which affects situations dealing with security and fitting into society. The Seeker Self seems more akin to Jupiter and Uranus, both related to the drive for independence and a separation from society's demands. Untimely events are more likely related to Uranus, while the inner drive for freedom is ruled by Jupiter. Changes, regardless of the cause, always bring growth.

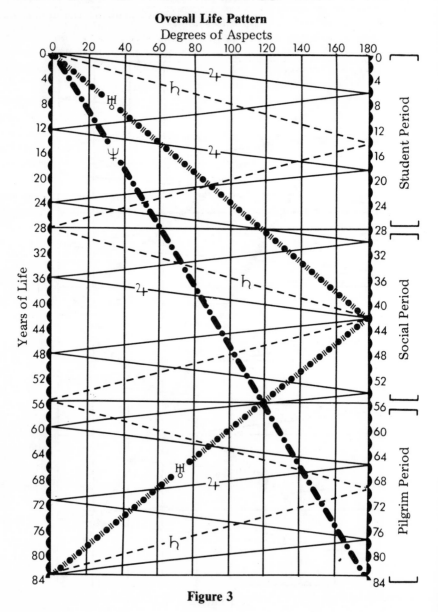

Figure 3

The graph of the first years from Birth to Puberty, Figure 2, is really a microcosm of the entire life span, shown in Figure 3 as Overall Life Pattern. Jupiter highlights the earlier period while Uranus overshadows the entire lifespan graph. The seven Martian cycles hold an important position in the early years, whereas the seven Jupiter cycles replace this activity in the Overall Life Pattern. The three early cycles of the Asteroids are replaced by the three major cycles of Saturn in the Overall Life Pattern. Thus, correlations between the growth and energy of Jupiter and Mars is seen, as well as similarities to structure and discipline with the Asteroids and Saturn. The influence of Saturn, representing the outer world, increases in effect during the Birth to Puberty period at the same rate as Neptune's spiritual influence increases during the Overall Life Pattern.

Since the first fourteen years might well be called the first Jupiter Cycle it could be used to define the concepts and meanings of separating and approaching aspects to natal positions of the same planets. In other words, all aspects relate to that transiting planet's aspect to its natal position, not to other transiting planetary positions. The natal position is represented by conjunction or zero on the graphs. Of course, relationships with other planets will temper the cyclic meaning in all cases. By comparing the keywords given in Table I, Major and Minor Aspects, with the delineations

Major and Minor Aspects

Aspect	Degrees	Waxing or Separating	Degree	Waning or Approaching
Conjunction	0	Unity	360	New Beginnings
Vigintile	18	Launching	342	Culmination
Semi-Oktil	22½	Speed Up	337½	Slow Down
Quindecile	24	Momentum	336	Braking
Semi-Sextile	30	Emergence	330	Integration
Decile	36	Resources	324	Support
Novile	40	Development	320	Nurturing
Semi-Square	45	Upsets	315	Stresses
Septile	51 3/7	Focusing	308 4/7	Commitment
Sextile	60	Opportunity	300	Application
Quintile	72	Insight	288	Talent/Transformation
Square	90	Major Crisis	270	Tests
Biseptile	102 6/7	Zeal	257 1/7	Dedication
Tredecile	108	Cornerstone	252	Unfoldment
Trine	120	Expansion	240	Blending/Absorption
Sesqui-Quadrate	135	Difficulties	225	Agitation
Biquintile	144	Advantage	216	Perception
Quincunx	150	Dilemma	210	Revision
Triseptile	154 2/7	Collective Need Considered	205 5/7	Cooperation
Opposition	180	Encounter	180	Repolarization

Table I

of the Jupiter cycle for the Birth to Puberty years the use of keywords for major and minor aspects will be shown.

Jupiter expands patterns. From age nine to 24 months the child launches into new surroundings and begins to walk and talk, thus actively gaining momentum and emerging as a functioning being. He develops resources, has brief upsets such as potty training, but continues to focus on opportunities for growth. The animal instinct or insight for survival is evident through the so-called "Terrible Twos." Around three years of age he faces the first test or major crisis of identity. In olden times this was the age for weaning from the mother's breast and being taken to be raised by the Amah or Nanny. Recognizing that he or she is not alone in the world the child begins to interrelate with playmates or siblings. Today this procedure is often accomplished by the introduction of nursery school experiences.

Zeal for living lays the cornerstone for further expansion in various creative activities. During this period most children learn the alphabet and some easy reading. The difficulties and advantages balance so that a five-year-old faced with the dilemma of kindergarten and leaving mother each morning begins to accept his fate. There he deals with collective need versus personal desire.

Around six or seven, when Jupiter reaches its first opposition to the natal placement, the child encounters the first real growth step in formal education. Some educators feel that this is the beginning of society's effort to stifle true creativity. During this stage the child learns cooperation, meaning a need to revise selfish patterns or else be punished. He perceives a greater scope of the world than previously held; in many countries children of this age are sent away to boarding schools. There is some agitation before true blending with his new environment is achieved.

When Jupiter and Saturn aspect together for the first time, around nine years of age, there is the realization of the unfoldment of responsibility, the cornerstone of responsible action. Seemingly simple action such as juggling a schedule of homework, Cub Scout meetings, music lessons and baseball practice, show his or her dedication to the group or sport followed by tests of his zealousness. Individual crises emerge throughout this period and are channeled into creative endeavors during pre-puberty. Commitment takes the form of practice or training resulting in stresses or conflicts. By accepting these simple responsibilities children are being nurtured, not spoiled, into maturity. Objective guidance or support given by teachers and coaches is more helpful now than family emotional involvement. Around age eleven or twelve the young animal is almost integrated into society and has begun to control or brake his personal freedom culminating in a new cycle of learning or expansion.

This whole Jupiter cycle could almost be called one of domestication and physical growth. Junior High School years are the transition to beginning a new period of mental and physical expression. Both Jupiter and Uranus exemplify the Seeker Self in this capacity.

In addition to Jupiter, the other planets are having their effects simultaneously. Saturn energies are often described as lessons, structuring, restrictions or conformity. However, the psychic Edgar Cayce mentioned that Saturn represents changes in life required to teach certain information and called Uranus the planet of extremes. Teacher or parent best describes the role of Saturn during the earliest stages of life. See Table II, Outer Earth Echoes, to follow the cycles of planets outside the Earth's orbit.

Outer Earth Echoes

Planet	Cycles in Life	Life Pattern
Mars	7	½ Saturn Cycle
Ceres (Asteroids)	3	1 Jupiter Cycle
Jupiter	7	1 Uranian or Life Cycle
Saturn	3	1 Uranian or Life Cycle
Uranus	1	1 Uranian or Life Cycle
Neptune	½	1 Uranian or Life Cycle

Table II

While analyzing the first fourteen years on the Birth to Puberty graph, Saturn first aspects its natal position about 18 months of age when the baby is learning such things as touching hot stoves to test parental warnings. The emergence, at about age two, of a separate being who may be allowed alone for brief intervals develops the resources. When parents stifle this developmental period they are creating further dependency patterns harmful to both child and parent. The three-year-old growth period includes maturation of teeth and bones, both Saturn concerns.

Through just punishment now the young individual learns to focus on right action versus wrong behaviour. Between four and five years of age the child is usually given more privileges such as riding a small bicycle, tending a pet and simple home chores. Practical insight begins to develop around age five, when he or she is exposed to the opinions of friends and fellow students.

The first Saturn test of responsibility occurs around six or seven when public school begins. Zeal for added responsibilities builds the cornerstone needed later in life. Insignificant as these events may seem, this is the basis for later development of leadership and organizational capabilities. The realization of public deadlines is important.

During the period from 9 to 12 years of age, there is an expansion of duties, followed by solving difficulties and dilemmas which present themselves at various intervals. Some advantages which may be carried into later life are introduced during this period such as music lessons, swimming or skating, horseback riding, tennis or even the first part-time job. The child is coming to grips with fitting into the basic social structure in which he or she lives.

Cycles of Uranus begin to manifest around age five when there is a sudden change or disruption of routine brought about by forces outside the individual. Schedules and rules made by the school change the personal daily habits of eating, napping and even toilet patterns. When Uranus touches its first aspect, or separating vigintile, with natal Uranus it is truly launching changes in the life. At the same time the asteroid Ceres is in approaching vigintile aspect with its radix, giving a culmination or ending of the child's first cycle of training and structuring. Creativity develops through the next cycle, emerging as resourcefulness in arts and crafts. The child learns to focus through Uranian upsets thus gaining intuitive insight and knowledge into everyday routines.

Around age thirteen or fourteen physical changes are brought about by the onset of puberty with its accompanying hormone changes. Again, this timing is not developed by the individual, but set by hereditary and environmental factors. Uranus normally brings disconcerting changes from outside the control of the personality.

Slowly the Neptune influence begins to be felt by the child about nine or ten years of age with introduction from religious sources. Preparations for the traditional Bar Mitzvah or Confirmation began around this age. Many churches still use this for the time of serious study with the young people emerging as participating members of the religious community. Today's child also has the illusion or disillusion of television and motion pictures to evaluate. Even the drug problem seems to be related to this early age group.

To integrate these cycles at their first major blending of influences seems helpful. While Jupiter and Uranus have been expanding the creative endeavors through upsets and advantages, Saturn has been teaching the value of routine or structure. Neptune and Jupiter combine to give momentum in religious encounters followed by integration into the customs of the family or society. Puberty is the first Saturn peak, adding responsibilities through encounters with others. Added concerns are necessary to develop stamina and depth of character. Some previously innocent playfulness may now have dire consequences because of the body changes. Jupiter, as well as Mars, in sextile positions to their respective radix positions add opportunities for growth and physical maturity. Life in the teens can be fun if responsibility is accepted first. Uranian demands for change have been discussed. Accepting these changes or extremes as inevitable and making the best use of them creates less confusion than rebelliousness. As mentioned, Neptune brings the emergence of moral and religious values.

By adding the two-year Mars energy cycles to the graph, periods of acceleration are highlighted. Not surprisingly, this energy explains some of the periods of expansion and opportunities as well as difficulties and strife.

8

During the first 23 years physical energies are diminished near the odd-year birthdays because Mars is transiting opposite its natal position. Which, of course, means there is more stamina and impetus to initiate or complete projects during the even-numbered years, from birth to 23. Because Mars completes its orbit in 23 months there will be the loss of a year every 12 cycles or 23 years. Between ages of 23 and 46 the high-energy patterns will be during the odd years, less energy during the even years, returning to the birth pattern around age 46. Since Mars cycles are so frequent they will deal more with daily matters than the greater life-cycle pattern. These cycles seem to have greater relevance in the early years.

The combined effects of the Asteroids seem to fit into a four to five year cycle which has been shown in the Birth to Puberty Graph. They deal with establishing routines, daily patterns and diet, general health and relationships. These cycles are replaced by the Saturn cycles in the Overall Life Pattern. Further study is necessary before more effects of the Asteroids may be shown.

Pluto has not been considered in this analysis because its motion is so erratic that it does not fit into any of the mathematical patterns. For further indication, the basic Bode's Law and Sidereal Periods are given in Table III. The planet predicted and charted by Sevin and Landscheidt, named Transpluto or Bacchus, is mentioned because it does fit part of the pattern. Little is known of its meaning or effects, astronomically or astrologically.

Patterns

	Bode's Law, A.U.		Sidereal Periods	
	Proposed	Actual	Proposed	Actual
Earth	1	1	1 Year	1 Year
Mars	1.6	1.5	2 Years	23 Months
Ceres (Asteroids)	2.8	2.8	5 Years	55 Months
Jupiter	5.2	5.2	12 Years	11.88 Years
Saturn	10.0	9.5	30 Years	29.42 Years
Uranus	19.6	19.2	75 Years	83.75 Years
Neptune	38.8	30.6	188 Years	163.74 Years
Pluto	—	Variable	—	245.33 Years
Transpluto	77.2	77.7	470 Years	686 Years
Unknown Outer Planet	154	—	1175 Years	—

Table III

Visually the entire life pattern falls naturally into three similar sections represented by the three major Saturn cycles. Interestingly, the Hindus consider the first 29 or 30 years of life as the Student Period, the next thirty as the Social Period and the last thirty as the Pilgrim Period. This same term or years of training and study was accepted by ancient Judaic laws. A man was not considered an adult until age 30. Both of these concepts are dealing with Saturn cycles or the time it takes for Saturn to return to its natal position.

Figure 2 shows completed in detail one-half of the first Saturn cycle. The influence of Mars and the Asteroids will recede further into the background as ingrained patterns and habits, functioning much as the percussion instruments in an orchestra give supportive rhythm, as the larger planets make themselves more audible. Jupiter completes yet another cycle of growth more on the level of mental expansion and relationship experiences than physical growth. Saturn begins its return to the radix through the end of the teens and the early twenties. Approaching Saturn squares its natal placement near the twenty-first birthday which was originally decreed the Age of Maturity in this country. At the same time, Jupiter squares natal Jupiter and Uranus attains its first square to natal Uranus. Truly a time of major decisions; one of the most trying of the Marker Events. Neptune is even in semi-square to its natal position giving further upsets and deceptions. The Asteroids are shown forming yet another square. This is a difficult period when young people truly break the emotional and economic umbilical cords, leaving them to face life's tests alone. Perhaps society is being kind to release some responsibilities at the new Age of Legality, 18. Yet Jupiter opposing natal Jupiter at 18 decreases some opportunities for expansion. More supportive aspects are available when the individual reaches the ages of 23 through 27 as Jupiter, Saturn and Neptune leave the major aspects for Uranian initiative. This phenomenon may explain why more people are earning advanced degrees before establishing their permanent careers.

As Saturn returns to its natal position, with Jupiter and Uranus trining to open doors to expansion and opportunities, the first re-evaluation of life's purpose begins. How much easier to realize that all which has gone before has been merely training for life's productive period. This time of new beginnings should be a period of joy and expectancy, not of doubt and soul searching. Society, in deciding that a permanent career and home be established before the end of Saturn's first return, has merely been working at odds with life's basic harmonies.

Between ages thirty and sixty was declared the Social Period by ancient Indian astrologers. But they did not mean parties and amusements, rather the time of life dedicated to the betterment of humanity through success in one's chosen field of endeavor, raising and training a family, caring for ageing parents and aiding others in need, as well as preparing for a financially secure old age. Feeling that the thirties are so vital to success is not necessary if an individual realizes that ten years will neither determine reward nor failure in the long run. Whether or not one is elected to the Junior League or becomes Vice President before forty is relatively unimportant in the greater scope of things. Important contributions to humanity are made at all ages, even after death.

Emma Belle Donath

On the Overall Life Pattern the visual similarity found between the Student and Pilgrim Periods is missing in the vital bridge of the Social Period. All cycles lead to a cresting or turning point in the middle of the graph, or Middle Age. Thirty-five seems to be the inner Developmental Phase for insight into the changes to occur in this mid-period. While Jupiter, Neptune and Saturn also form quintile aspects to their respective natal positions, Uranus at quincunx demands a revision of earlier concepts. Many persons begin to explore their subconscious minds and react to this new phase in various ways. Here the seeds are planted which will mature at the end of the second Saturn cycle.

As middle life grows and develops the Uranian influence becomes stronger, to culminate between ages 40 and 45 with the Uranus opposition to its natal position. Simultaneously both Jupiter and Saturn are opposite their natal placements, while Neptune has reached its first square to natal Neptune. This major change will not take place overnight nor will all the crises manifest at once. The personality is at its furthest point from the natal ego, so the individual may act completely unlike him- or herself. Whether this period will be influenced by deceit or illusion depends on the preparations taken prior to the years of decision. This is the time of many divorces, career changes, regional moves, unexpected babies, sex-reversals, religious conversions and realigning of loyalties. Whether the changes are for better or worse depends on the individual and his or her goals. Some people get a new start on life with understanding companionship while others go toward physical and financial ruin.

The graph leading away from this major opposition at age 42 follows the pattern found inside the Great Pyramid of Cheops in Egypt. There are three major influences all going to the same point at the end of this Saturn cycle, or retirement. The Path of Monetary Growth, or the Jupiter line, leads to the later test of possessiveness around age 45. Those facing this test must rid themselves of physical possessions or proceed to decline to the Jupiter conjunction at age 48 sometimes called Gluttony or Saturation. The only way out of these depths is complete transformation in the early fifties when nature even provides a physical hormone change. The period of menopause, which decreases both the estrogen supply in the female and the testosterone level in the male, gives an opportunity to blend into more harmonious understanding of the roles of each other. This does not so much concern sexual activity as a more equal sharing of the female passiveness and male aggressiveness.

On the Path of Security, Materialism and Renown, or Saturn line, the zeal of dedication can lead to changes or depression during this entire cycle. Uranus represents the Path of Eccentricity which expresses agitation with more worldly and successful people in the early fifties, leading to a later possible encounter. By not detouring, this path may be followed straight to true spiritual expansion or complete deceit at the second Saturn return around 56 to 60. So often the meaning of life is lost when this middle period is considered as the completion rather than the bridge of life.

The three major periods are reminiscent of the phases of life of the Vestal Virgins in ancient Greece. Their first ten years in the temples were spent in training or preparation to perform their duties. During the next ten years these ladies shined candlesticks, lighted the sacred fires, mended the tapestries and cared for the holy vessels according to the manner in which they had been trained. For their third and last ten years of service the Virgins were teachers of the young novices.

An interesting experiment was carried out by abutting the first and third Saturn cycles together from Figure 3. Jupiter returned from a trine position to conjunction with natal Jupiter without facing a third encounter, or opposition. Saturn began a completely new cycle uninterrupted. The Uranus line continued as Neptune influence without a gap or jump. Only the early Neptune line was left without continuity. Are these years of the middle period only tests of development for the Neptune or spiritual influence? The point of conjunction is where the traditional point of adulthood begins.

The last Saturn cycle is related to the Path of the Pilgrim when all worldly affairs are completed. The last vestiges of fame and title are handed on to sons and daughters who in their turn will take up the burdens of society and family. As Jupiter returns to its natal position around age sixty the pilgrim prepares for the coming decline of monetary resources. Since this coincides with Saturn's separation from its radix, the investing or sorting may be done wisely, as storing grain in times of plenty for times of famine. However, when the greater scope of purpose is not perceived, a miserly attitude may begin at this point increasing throughout the rest of the life. Many elderly persons have shown tendencies to hoard such worthless items as used newspapers, outgrown or worn out clothing, even spoiled food, when this Jupiter and Saturn influence is not properly understood.

Around ages 63 to 65 Jupiter, Saturn and Uranus all square their natal positions predicting major tests and crises which manifest physically as the Marker Event of retirement. Whether or not the difficulties intimated by Neptune's sesquiquadrate to its radix create emotional trauma or increase the faith depends on individual attitudes.

For some persons the later period of life will again emphasize the smaller Martian and Asteroid cycles of health, daily routine and minor details. The increasing Neptune influence will then be received more as disillusionment or fear of deceit than as unfoldment of greater Universal Truths. Persons between ages 60 and 90 may repeat the first Saturn cycle in reverse, going from adolescence backwards into childhood or senility. The choice belongs to each man or woman, whether to make egg-carton wastebaskets in the recreation room of a nursing home or to make such contributions to humanity as did Grandma Moses.

During the last Saturn cycle there are many periods where the aspects can bring the end of the physical body. The quantity of aspects during the last opposition of Saturn to its natal position in the early seventies often manifests either as death or physical decline. Man is his own most severe judge and may determine his worthlessness at this critical self-evaluation period. Here there is little difference between the so-called workaholic and the alcoholic. Both have escaped the real necessity of life, facing one's inner self to learn that the only true freedom or achievement comes from within, not from without.

At this same time Neptune is in quincunx aspect, showing concern with health problems. Though Jupiter and Uranus are both in sextile aspect they are approaching conjunction, meaning more application of resources than opening of new doors at this age. The final unfoldment of responsible action coincides with the last cornerstone of expansive action in the mid-seventies.

Mental decline or withdrawal may happen at the last Jupiter quincunx and opposition aspects during the late seventies. Saturn comes to its last culminating square while Uranus is coasting toward its radix with a semi-sextile. Neptune releases its last functioning aspect after age 72 until it reaches opposition in the early eighties, forcing a test of faith for almost a full decade. Without the influence of Neptune the native may feel either devoid of all sense of softness and gentleness typified by the term "rose-colored glasses" or, more seriously, may feel separated from his or her religious source of inspiration.

For persons who survive the tests of this first Uranian cycle, the title of Sage is bestowed during the following Period of Sainthood.

Cycles may be used not so much for precise astrological timing but to see the undergirding influences during various periods of life. Certain transiting influences would not be interpreted in the same manner during the Student Period as during the Pilgrim Period. Changes indicated during the Middle Period might be further explained by progressed aspects. This is merely an overview of life using the minor aspects as well as major ones to explain certain stages.

2

Simple Procedure for Locating Aspects

After calculating planetary positions in the regular manner for a natal horoscope, place the planets on the 360-degree wheel given in Figure 4. This wheel may be duplicated for repeated usage. A Natal Horoscope Calculation form is included in Appendix A. Use of a straight edge or small ruler is helpful in placing planets as near as possible their exact zodiacal degree in the wheel.

360 Degree Wheel

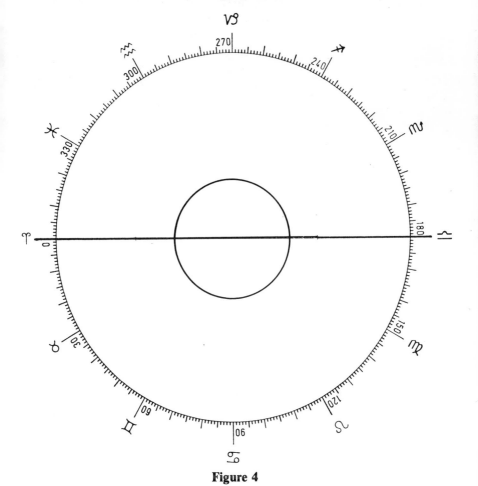

Figure 4

15

In each chapter concerning a particular aspect a 360-degree wheel similar to the one found in Figure 5 is included. The major or minor aspect considered is marked by lines on either side of the arrow. By following the steps given determine whether or not the aspect under discussion is found in each chart. Use only a 1 or 2 degree orb for all minor aspects. For major aspects, use the orb described in the text being used for that is how the research was followed.

1. Place planets on outer rim of a 360-degree wheel,
2. Cut out, or duplicate, the aspect wheel to be used,
3. Place the aspect wheel over the natal wheel, securing at center dot,
4. Place arrow of aspect wheel on the planet being considered,
5. Look to see whether any planets are positioned at the ends of one or both of the other lines shown on aspect wheel,
6. Read the interpretation given for said aspect between two planets in the appropriate chapter of this book.

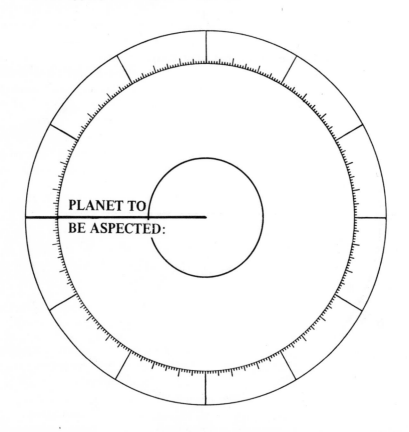

PLANET TO
BE ASPECTED:

Aspect Wheel Example
Figure 5

3

Basic Planetary Energies

Although many books have been written concerning the energies of planets in this solar system it is wise to include a few words about the general concepts used in this particular research. One of the best sources for understanding planetary energies is an ancient myth or fairy tale about the legendary god or goddess for whom that planetary body is named. Another source is the scientific reports, or astronomical data, concerning that particular body. No astrological premise will work which does not also agree with the physical attributes of that solar body.

As previously explained, only planetary energies were considered in this volume so that it can be of equal usage to both Tropical and Sidereal astrologers.

Moon or Luna: Because of the position of the Moon as a satellite of the Earth it is, of course, to persons living on Terra important. As moons of other planets are discovered and discussed in the newspapers, magazines and bulletins it might be well to begin calling this little body by its ancient name of Luna in order to determine which energy is involved. Only in geocentric astrology is Luna considered because only from the Earth's surface would it be considered to have significant influence. Phases of the Moon or Luna affect mankind and all living creatures on this globe in a cyclic sense. Because this body reflects the light of the Sun it represents the opposite factors from the Sun.

Glyph: ☽
Keywords for Moon or Luna:

body fluids	fluctuation	inherent	open receptacle
changes	general public	insulating	receptive
ebb and flow	habits	lack of self restraint	
everyday affairs	hallucinations	lower mind	recessive
fairy castles	heredity	memory	subjective
feeling	imagination	moody	sympathetic
feminine	inconsistent	mother	women

Lilith or Dark Moon: One of the dark moons of the Planet Earth, Lilith is three times as far from Earth as Luna. Multi-dimensional, like a many faceted diamond, Lilith's influence is felt on all planes. Positive aspects are denied until the lessons of Saturn are learned. Conjunctions, trines and sextiles are the most subversive at present as people willingly respond to the siren's call. Lilith is important in the horoscopes of mystics and psychics. It may show the timing of soul's age. Further information on this body may be found in *Lilith, the Doodler,* by Lois Daton. Because of continuing research on this body delineations will not be given in a separate chapter but limited to keywords presented here.

Glyph: ⚸
Keywords for Lilith:

advancement	exaggeration	misinterpretation	self-undoing
bad timing	excess	misty	separation
catastrophe	fascination	mysterious	shadow
compulsion	hidden	pondering	susceptibility
darkness	infatuation	retribution	temptations
depth	lack	sacrifice	veiled
disruptive	miscalculation	selflessness	violent

Sun or Helios: The Sun and Earth positions are exactly opposite each other in a horoscope. The Sun is not really a planet, but actually a solar star, so many of the characteristics which are normally attributed to the Sun actually belong to the planet Earth or Terra. Excepting this concept are the life-giving energies sent out from the Sun to all planets in this system as well as its Sun spots which disrupt all forms of communications. They could be said to represent the anger of the Sun.

Glyph: ☉
Keywords for Sun or Helios:

body	glory	objectivity	seed
cell of physical body	health	physical	solar logos
dignity	heart	radiance	spirit
dominant people	honor	renown	triumph
dynamic	life-force	right	vitality
father	masculine	rulership	will to live

Mercury: Mercury was Messenger of the Gods; Lord of Divine Books; Lord of Divine Word; God of Letters, Science, Mathematics and Wisdom; and Carrier of the Serpent or Kundalini Fire. This son of Jupiter and Maia was known as Hermes to the Egyptians and Greeks, Wotan by the Germans, Nebo in Chaldea and the Indian Buddha. From earliest childhood Mercury was in constant motion bringing new ideas where his feet touched

Earth. Ever youthful he continued to translate the rules and commands of the gods for mortal minds.

Glyph: ☿
Keywords for Mercury:

abstracts	bronchial tubes	impulsive	speaks
adapts	businessman	journalism	teachers
agility	catalyst	joy	telephones
alert	cerebrospinal nerves	limbs	thyroid
analysis	charming	lower mind	tongue
aware	communicates	mischevious	transmission
biases	comprehension	moves	twinning
books	debates	nervous	vocal cords
breathe	dexterity	pickpockets	writing

Venus: The question in dealing with this planetary energy is whether it really is Venus or Aphrodite. Venus was wife of Vulcan, mother to Cupid, mistress and finally consort to her husband's brother Mars, daughter of Jupiter and Dione, and chosen as the fairest of the goddesses by mortal Paris. Her golden girdle gave such an air of beauty, grace and elegance that all who came near fell in adoration at her feet. Plato gave to this goddess the title of Venus Popularia and called the older, more mysterious one, Venus Urania because she was reported to have sprung from the froth of the sea where Uranus's mutilated genitals were tossed. The parentless goddess Aphrodite better examplifies the esoteric Lord of the Higher Mind or Goddess of Beauty and Light than Venus. Romans and Hebrews called this deity Lucifer when she rose as the Morning Star.

Glyph: ♀
Keywords for Venus:

abstract thought	charm	furs	refinement
adroit	color	incense	sentiment
affection	decorations	jewelry (real)	sister
appetites	dishevelment	luxuries	sloth
appreciation	dove	ovaries	sympathy
artistic	estrogen	parathyroid	taste
beauty	fatty tissue	peace	veins
cellulose	flirtations	pleasure	women

Earth or Terra: Gaea was the old mother of all including the sky represented by her son-husband Uranus with whom she united to populate the heavens, ocean and earth. Other names for this goddess include Roman Tallus, Indian Tara, Egyptian Isis or Nat, and Greek Ge, Te or Terra. Earth is the sure foundation or the solid base. Positioned exactly opposite the Sun many of the attributes of the Sun are really reactions of the Earth. Terra Firma is concerned with where man can experience reactions and relationships.

Glyph: $\oplus$
Keywords for Earth or Terra:

alive	courage	fulcrum point	reflective
apply	duality	healing	restorative
balances	evolving	interdependence	seasonal
benign	dense	intense	supportive
bluish-green	diffusion	maternal	sustaining
compromise	fertile	possessive	womb

Mars: This son of Jupiter and Juno was brother to both Vulcan and Hebe, lover of Venus, God of War and Husbandry, whose duty it was to dispel terror and fear. Mars was always depicted as handsome but vain, ever ready to rush into battle. Bloodshed and weaponry were common symbols of Mars whose other names included Greek Ares, Scandanavian Froh, Christian St. George, Chaldean Nergal and the Babylonian God of War and Pestilence. In earlier days Mars also portrayed the wise farmer who culled his flocks and grains in order to provide for his family and village.

Glyph: ♂
Keywords for Mars:

action	challenge	hasten	nose
adventure	chivalry	honor	policeman
adrenalin	drive	injury	red
anger	energy	iron	survival
ardent	fever	knife	tools
athletics	force	lover	virility
brother	gall bladder	martial	will power
bestiality	gymnastics	mechanization	work

Ceres or Demeter: Daughter of Saturn and Rhea; sister of Zeus, Pluto, Poseidon, Vesta and Juno; Ceres was concerned with planting seeds as well as being the Goddess of Harvest, Goddess of Caves and Underground Springs, and Celtic Danna. She was often the one who committed the offering to the knife rather than the victim. Here is another of the mothering principles, devoid of emotionalism.

Glyph: ?

Keywords for Ceres:

adoption	digestion	instinct	pigs
ant	draperies	intestines (upper)	practical
antiseptic	ecology	habits	protective
austerity	fairs	harvest	salutary laws
bread	farm	laxatives	scythe
cereal	folded clothes	laundry	springs
civilizing	harvest	menses	toilet
clothes chest	honey	nurse	warts
domesticate	hospitals	nurture	wounds

Pallas Athena: Athens was named for this benefactress who gave olive trees to Greece. Pallas Athena, Goddess of Wisdom, was born from her father's brow fully dressed and armed. The daughter of Zeus and Themis (whom Zeus swallowed) was also Goddess of Cities and Defense. Pallas trains the energy which Mars has so abundantly. She was known as a great breaker and tamer of the horses which warriors rode into battle.

Glyph: ⚲

Keywords for Pallas Athena:

allocate	earnest	liaison	shield
armor	crusader	library	skills
bartering	employment	mathematics	trigger
beetle	flute	noble	uniforms
bravery	guardian	owl	valiant
conservation	handicrafts	pattern	vocation
counsel	independent	sculptor	wisdom
cunning	iris	spinning	women's rights

Juno: Rightful wife of Jupiter, Juno was also his sister, through their parentage of Saturn and Rhea. She was known as Goddess of Maternity and Marriage, concerned with childbirth, matrons and ceremonies. Keeper of the Mint, the only married goddess on Mt. Olympus, Juno was frustrated by her lack of actual power. Juno, or Greek Hera, was a beautiful but jealous wife who spent much of her time and energy restoring her youthful charms.

Glyph: ⚵

Keywords for Juno:

bee	contraceptives	eggs	keys
birth (happy)	co-ruler	etiquette	lilies
bossy	cosmetics	fidelity	marriage
bride	documents	host/hostess	migraines
coiffure	eccentric	jeweled	nosey

ornamentation	pharmacist	sceptre	uptight
protocol	reflected glory	shrewd	vindictive
parties	restrictive	subtle	wiles
perpetuating	salves	treasurer	yoke

Vesta: As eldest daughter of Saturn and Rhea the goddess Vesta or Hestia was sister to reigning Jupiter. She remained a virgin and was considered Goddess of the Sacred Fires of the Temple and Hearth. In Greece this deity was called Hestia. Vestal Virgins of the temple service were named for this goddess of devotion.

Glyph: ⊻

Keywords for Vesta:

acolyte	cultural heritage	hearth	spider
altar	dedicated	kiln fired	stability
archives	deer	laurel	traditions
candles	fanatic	masks	tripod
ceramics	geneology	period of servitude	warmth
cleansing	graves	sanctuary	zealous

Jupiter: Youngest son of Saturn and Rhea, Jupiter released his brothers who had been swallowed by their father at birth. He perpetuated the policy begun by his father when Saturn castrated his own parent, Uranus. Jupiter, or Greek Zeus, ruled on Mt. Olympus along with his siblings and the children of his many matings. In dividing the universe Pluto took the Underworld and Action, Neptune ruled the Sea and Love with Emotion, leaving Jupiter the Earth and Sky along with Wisdom and Thought. Some of Jupiter's other titles are Christian St. Peter, Pantheon Marduk and Hindu Brahmanaspati.

Glyph: ♃

Keywords for Jupiter:

abundance	ethics	joviality	priest
arteries	excess	judge	publishing
benevolence	expand	liver	seer
bigotry	favoritism	magnetic	status
blood plasma	fortune	massive	thunderbolt
civil servant	funeral	middle age	turbulence
culture	gall secretion	philosophy	turquoise
ennobling	influential	pituitary gland	universality

Saturn: This son of Uranus and Gaea castrated his father thus taking the life-giving force from Uranus. Then Saturn became father of Jupiter and the inhabitants of Mt. Olympus following his period as ruler of the universe for the Golden Age. The deity Saturn has been called Lord of Karma, Dweller on the Threshold, Throat Chakra of the Solar Logos, true husband and Old Father Time. Mother Nature punished Saturn through his youngest son for not sharing the earth's bounty with his children and his monstrous Cyclops brothers.

Glyph: ♄
Keywords for Saturn:

administrator	concentration	hearing	schedules
ageing	contraction	nest	serious
alienation	dentistry	orders	severe
authority	discipline	organizes	skeleton
banishment	examinations	parental	skin
bone	fences	pessimism	stones
character	form	quilt	teeth
coldness	grades	restrictions	trials

Uranus: Oldest of the known gods Uranus married Gaea and bred many children including the Cyclops, the Titans and various monsters. He was then mutilated by son Saturn who took over rulership of the heavens and the earth. Uranus was originally thought of as the sky who married the earth and shows enlarged dimensions of life or power above normal.

Glyph: ♅
Keywords for Uranus:

aloofness	dynamic	maverick	reform
authoritative	electric	modification	ruptures
autonomic nerves	engineers	mutation	spasmodic
capricious	experiments	nervous energy	uncharted
circulation	freedom	occult	unusual
conductivity	gadgets	oscillations	uranium
curious	impulsive	polarization	vibration
durable	insight	professional	willful

Neptune: As brother of Pluto and Jupiter, son of Saturn and Rhea, Neptune was a moody and violent god who raced over the waves in a chariot drawn by a team of white horses. Neptune ruled the oceans which entitled him to create earthquakes at his caprice. He was second in command only to brother Jupiter.

Glyph: ♆

Keywords for Neptune:

addict	chemists	filters	mirrors
alcohol	coma	fish	mystery
amnesia	curiosity	fluids	paralysis
aura	dreams	gas	odors
body tissues	electromagnetic	hypnotic	radiation
camouflage	enchantment	inspires	sailor
chaotic	enzymes	intrigue	spy
compassion	fantasy	lyden glands	trance

Pluto: The gods forged a cloak of invisibility for Pluto which allowed him to capture his victims sight unseen to be taken to his underground kingdom. For this son of Saturn and Rhea ruled the underworld and action, leaving the earth and sky to brother Jupiter. Pluto once stole pretty, young Persephone from her mother Ceres and caused chaos with the growing seasons of the earth for a year.

Glyph: ♇

Keywords for Pluto:

analyst	fanaticism	plumbers	toxin
atomic fusion	gangster	regeneration	transform
blackmail	invisible changes	reproductive	tyranny
body PH	masses	revelation	unfoldment
cataclysm	meditation	sex appetites	upheaval
excretory	metamorphosis	subconscious	urethra
detective	neurosis	surgeon	underworld
faddish	perineum	swaying	victims

Transpluto or Bacchus: Bacchus was the legendary God of Wine ruling lavishly over feasts and festivals sharing merriment with all who joined him. He represents, on the other hand, the Communion Wine of the Resurrection. John Robert Hawkins has written a comprehensive book on this as yet undiscovered planet in our solar system. Hawkins's book is titled *Transpluto or Shall We Call Him Bacchus?*

Glyph: ♹

4

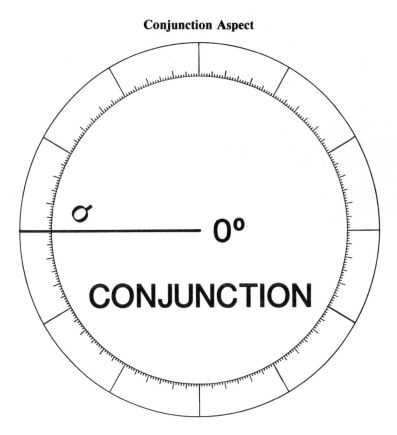

Conjunction Aspect

σ

0°

CONJUNCTION

When two or more planets are positioned near each other in the heavens they are called Conjunct or in Conjunction Aspect. The closer their positions the more potent this blending of energies. Because the planets travel at varying speeds the faster moving planets move into Conjunction with the slower moving planets so that one body is always aspecting another body. Sometimes this visit is brief, like the postman leaving mail and quickly departing. At other times slower moving planets may linger with each other like the proverbial "man who came to dinner" and stayed for a year. In either case the changes wrought may be grand or minor. The telegram bringing bad news will be no less shocking because of its brevity than the smoldering fire of chared ruins of the parental home.

At each period when two planets Conjunct each other they both complete an old cycle of activity for those two energies and simultaneously set the stage for a new round of emphasis. This can be likened to the revolving door found in commercial establishments such as banks and department stores. Entering the empty section from either inside the store or outside you then must travel in a set direction through the enclosure until reaching the opposite opening of the doors. The time spent within the door apparatus is like the period when planets are in Conjunction. This is both leaving an old space and entering a new area at the same time. Whether you move backward or forward makes little difference, travel must occur in one direction or another to be released from the enclosure. During the period in the enclosure there are both the seeds of the beginning and the roots of the ending, as in the Yin-Yang symbol. So it is with planets in Conjunction aspect.

Each planet in Conjunction tends to bring out the characteristics of the other planet. When these energies are compatible there is a blending. However, some planets seem to be naturally antagonistic to each other so Conjunctions with them bring aggressive behavior. All astrologers seem to agree on the point that planets in Conjunction display their strongest reactions of each other.

There are many volumes containing multiple delineations for planets in Conjunction so this text will only contain the above discussion and the following keywords.

Glyph: ☌
Keywords of the Conjunction:

action	direction	initiates	pioneering
beginnings	dynamics	intensifies	power
consolidation	emphasis	newness	prominence
cyclic	focalizing	personal	unity

5

Vigintile Aspect

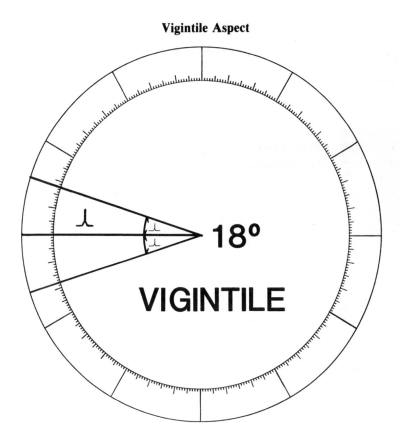

18°

VIGINTILE

The 18-degree angle or Vigintile is formed by a division of the 360-degree circle into twenty equal portions. This seldom used aspect tends to bring issues to a conscious awareness whether by launching ideas as one planet begins to separate from a slower-moving solar body or by culminating action as the planets approach the next period of togetherness. As its energies are subtle they are often ignored or passed over as residual effects of a wide-orb conjunction.

When this aspect is considered from the esoteric viewpoint it is called the door between two worlds determined by the planets involved. Some occultists call it the psychic or spiritual door through which the disciple can reach an inner world of Soul or the subconscious.

Interpretations given to this aspect by Frances Sakoian and Louis Acker in their books *The Minor Aspects* and *Major and Minor Approaching and Separating Aspects* include to tap resources, to apply will and transcend and to relate.

From the research done in preparing this text the term "innate understanding" applied most often when the 18-degree aspect was investigated. Of course, issues involved were determined by which planets were interacting. Some esoteric delineations given by Dr. Elisabeth V. Bacon of Columbus, Ohio, are also included in the planet to planet discussions with her permission.

For most accurate determination an orb of 1 to 2 degrees is used when interpreting the Vigintile aspect.

Glyph: ⅃

Keywords of the Vigintile:

awareness	culminating	launching	topping
benefits	doorway	rounding off	understanding
comprehending	initiating	sensitive	utilizing

Vigintiles of the Sun:

Sun Vigintile Moon — On one plane this native walks in the essence of what is called the true Spiritual Sun. In more mundane situations he or she focuses on intimate surroundings. This person is emotionally very sensitive but not sophisticated in ways of the world.

Sun Vigintile Mercury — Being subtle about expressing his or her own opinions this native normally exerts influence through another person. There is present the ability to blend old traditions with new behavioral patterns. Quite often this individual is forced to live a greater part of life away from the country of his birth and must, of necessity, become bilingual. Deep feelings will be moved in contacts with inner or spiritual worlds.

Sun Vigintile Venus — This person is given the wonderful gift to see the true beauty in all things. He or she understands the value and healing power of physical touch. Much of this understanding is held within a calm outer demeanor.

Sun Vigintile Mars — Direct contact makes the strongest impression on a person born with this natal aspect. He or she works at launching new concepts. Women with this energy like to revamp the current styles in dress. There may be occasions when these people will have direct supernatural or telepathic contacts.

Sun Vigintile Ceres — When this combination of energies appears in a natal horoscope it indicates that the native will reap benefits from seeds sown early in life. There is present the ability to utter deep philosophical comments which seem to flow through the individual.

Sun Vigintile Pallas Athena — This person understands current trends, especially in business affairs. Being goal oriented, he or she utilizes past mistakes in future planning. One who is so inclined can walk between two worlds with great gentleness and wisdom. This is a good aspect for a psychologist or psychiatrist.

Sun Vigintile Juno — Where the issues governed by these two planets are concerned this individual is a veritable paradox. At one point he or she will be most liberal, even to suggesting new opportunities for women in positions of leadership, while on other occasions he shows sustained prejudices against any change in the social status quo. A subtle aspect dealing with the native's manner of integrating into society.

Sun Vigintile Vesta — This person is resourceful in matters of the heart and capable of fully expressing great passion or compassion. There is an adhesive quality which enjoys getting people together on the spur of the moment.

Sun Vigintile Jupiter — Any contacts with the outside world will prove to be overwhelming adventures for this naive person. It is best to let them stand in awe of more sophisticated truths rather than attempt to involve him or her in an interpretation of the mechanics behind such activity. Overexposure to foreign conditions could bring on mental and emotional anguish.

Sun Vigintile Saturn — The inner or spiritual worlds challenge this native because he or she has not found the sensitivity and refinement expected in the outer life. There is a constant seeking whether through observing the various kingdoms of nature or through analyzing human behavior. From this searching attitude often springs the ability to relate such awareness so that others can understand it, thus creating an award-winning author or artist. Esoterically these people are being judged during the life span for past and present activities.

Sun Vigintile Uranus — With this combination of energies in the natal horoscope an individual often travels where others fear to even venture whether it be into outer space or into realms of innovative mind. This can be a very catalytic aspect causing other energies in the horoscope to be activated. Such a native may be said to be either an adept or a person who has attained a certain degree of mastership.

Sun Vigintile Neptune — Such an idealist with gentle eyes and a dreamy expression would hardly be thought to have the determination to carry out decisions as this native proves possible. Several of the individuals investigated lived a love story which will become legend in generations to come. All of them initiated freedom from obligations of power and authority to follow their own beliefs. This is an aspect strongly relating to works of science fiction, super-plane beings or such manifestations as UFO's.

Sun Vigintile Pluto — Constantly digging up old traditions or reminiscing about childhood pleasures leads people to consider this native as rather backward while just the opposite is true. It is through this search for meaning in the symbols of the past that he or she discovers value in signs of the present and future. There is a tendency to rely on the subconscious mind to understand the present. In this way liberation comes from the socially accepted principles of the moment to a more universal awareness.

Vigintiles of the Moon:

Moon Vigintile Mercury — This person becomes the spokesman for others who remain behind the scenes too emotionally involved to participate. He or she overcomes childhood shyness only out of strong feelings for some cause to which he can truly relate.

Moon Vigintile Venus — An idealist who wants all men to be emotional brothers this native paints or writes of such feelings with bold strokes of the brush or pen which sometimes shock more than they appeal. With an appealing outer appearance he or she draws people into his sphere of activity until they learn of the commitment which this individual expects of all his close associates. When friends drop away at this point the native becomes discouraged and distressed.

Moon Vigintile Mars — Being slapped down on the first attempt to launch a new idea is often the most helpful thing that can happen as this native soon learns in life. This delay gives the time to perfect the theory or project being initiated into a more useable and acceptable form. So it is with a sustained injury or illness, there is presented the time to explore and investigate without the pressures of producing. This is a good aspect for the enquiring mind of a research engineer or mathematician. Having this particular combination of energies gives the emotional determination to get up after the native has fallen or been knocked down and try again.

Moon Vigintile Ceres — Any prolonged experience with animals or plants gives a respect and understanding for nature's flow of energy. This can be used as a way of learning to control the physical body and being compassionate with the problems of those who have physical deformities. Esoterically this aspect gives psychic gifts which may be trained and used in various forms of healing. Even as a child this native will enjoy sitting on the ground and contemplating his or her surroundings.

Moon Vigintile Pallas Athena — Having this planetary combination in the natal horoscope makes it difficult for the native to work in areas with which he or she is not compassionately involved. It is a good aspect for one doing counseling or personnel placement. Often he or she prefers working at home to being in a more structured atmosphere.

Moon Vigintile Juno — Although this native conforms to the social standards of the day he or she advances new ideas through the traditional channels. Dressing and appearing quite ordinary he finds means of bringing new beliefs to conscious awareness. This person really does feel aware of two emotional pulls throughout life.

Moon Vigintile Vesta — When these two planetary energies are in 18-degree aspect in the natal horoscope there is a concern with clearing away obstructions. When plans are skillfully and correctly made putting them into action is easy. This native objects to wasteful use of any product.

Moon Vigintile Jupiter — This native handles large sums of money with very little previous concern. He or she jumps in to do a job which more experienced people will refuse. There is an innate understanding of how to handle large-scale enterprises. Emphasis is on reacting out of personal comprehension. This native usually is sought after and has many associates but few intimate friends.

Moon Vigintile Saturn — At various periods of life this person is required to face new responsibilities without much experience or training. He relies on childhood or past life memories to impulsively guide him or her through the task or trial. Often this native is launched directly from obscurity into fame and fortune.

Moon Vigintile Uranus — Such an inventor as this native will dream up many fresh concepts during a lifetime. Whether or not he completes or manufactures any of these inventions depends on other factors in the natal horoscope. Some individuals with such an aspect launched new and exciting means of communicating while others were found only to have revealing dreams.

Moon Vigintile Neptune — There is an ability to translate nebulous religious ideas into current meaning when this aspect is present in the natal chart. Whether this restating is in keeping with present thought or not determines whether the native's revelations are accepted or rejected. This does not in the least detract from the authenticity of this individual's perception. This aspect is most likely to manifest in preachers, healers, radical spokesmen, religious teachers and reformers to name a few.

Moon Vigintile Pluto — A real winner is this individual who has charisma over crowds. He or she is sensitive to the attitudes around him as a good actor or writer must be to achieve success.

Vigintiles of Mercury:

Mercury Vigintile Venus — This often found aspect occurs in the natal horoscopes of persons having pleasant, well-modulated voices for public speaking. This native is usually concerned with the use of color whether in clothing worn or designed or in tones used throughout a home. He or she seems extremely aware of the changing seasons of the year. There is the ability to know how to "play on the heart strings" of friends and acquaintances.

Mercury Vigintile Mars — Such a person draws upon a limitless source of energy to keep up with his or her ideas. There is a contagious enthusiasm

31

spread among those working in the vicinity of this native. Being easily bilingual, he or she is a capable negotiator or interpreter. This aspect shows an innovative mind.

Mercury Vigintile Ceres — Writings flow easily out of the pen of this native, usually without need of revision or rewriting. He or she is also a talented speaker with an extensive vocabulary. There is interest in learning other languages in order to understand various cultures in which people live.

Mercury Vigintile Pallas Athena — Whether this individual is a professional teacher or not he or she spends a greater part of each day imparting knowledge and wisdom to others. Another side of this aspect reveals a person who enjoys working with his or her hands to create pleasant accent pieces for the home or surroundings.

Mercury Vigintile Juno — A brief and concise writer this native has a wry sense of humor which can be misunderstood. He or she serves in small tasks. There is both an interest and ability to perform intricate maneuvers with the fingers, such as exhibited in making fine stitches in prize winning quilts or such as shown in inventing various sewing machines and devices. This individual can be a natural mimic when he desires to do so.

Mercury Vigintile Vesta — During maturity this native works around childhood fears and apprehension. He or she is often required to initiate action in the very field which he holds in awe. There is a disciplined mind which lets the body act without allowing emotions to show through.

Mercury Vigintile Jupiter — A natural comic this individual can become popular by using his or her innate abilities and talents. Blessed with romantic good looks and a charming voice he early develops a sophisticated and nonchalant approach in public. Actually this native is as gentle as a lamb and will go instantly to the aid of persons in trouble.

Mercury Vigintile Saturn — Having this aspect in the natal horoscope gives the ability to instinctively know what older people want to hear and discuss. His or her conventional appearance appeals to more mature friends and acquaintances. This very conscientious native lets himself be made fun of if it is in the interest of achieving his goal in life.

Mercury Vigintile Uranus — Such an innovative individual experiments with everything from mind control to electrical devices all the while intuitively knowing what is most fruitful for him or her. This aspect is comfortable for an educator or research scientist. Being outspoken there is always the urge to launch a controversial campaign just to see how people react.

Mercury Vigintile Neptune — Unusual methods of communicating come easily for the individual born with this natal aspect. Whether it be sending sound through the air waves or dealing with autistic children on a nonverbal basis this native eventually achieves a breakthrough by using his or her intuition and experimenting with ideas. It is as if there is truly a way of straddling two worlds of expression.

Mercury Vigintile Pluto — This native finds it most satisfying to counsel troubled people. He or she knows how to say the right things and find the most healing methods without formal training. There is usually present an interest in studying ancient philosophies in order to understand the mystical import.

Vigintiles of Venus:

Venus Vigintile Mars — Without being told this individual knows the strategic moves to make whether it be during an armed battle, a friendly chess game or a corporate struggle. There is a forceful style which knows how to handle violence or threats to himself or his allies. Even as a child this native has a decided interest in the mechanics of war and challenges. This same trait makes him or her good at editing written material.

Venus Vigintile Ceres — If it were possible the person with this natal combination of planets would feed the multitudes daily. He or she loves nothing better than to gather friends and family around a table loaded with tasty morsels. In the same manner, this is a good aspect for a spiritual teacher who enjoys sustaining the soul's growth. Outdoor camping and picnicing are joyful for this person.

Venus Vigintile Pallas Athena — This native likes to set things up to operate on their own so he or she can relax from the details of daily work schedule. Whenever possible this individual will add paintings, chair covers, plants or such items to make the office or store in which he works more attractive. With this aspect there is an inborn perception of blending colors for the most striking effect.

Venus Vigintile Juno — If not married to actual relatives this native will seek out a person with similar background and upbringing for a lifetime mating. Thus there is a feeling of companionship as well as emotional excitement in his permanent relationships. This same criterion is used in choosing close friends.

Venus Vigintile Vesta — Time is no obstacle when this individual is searching for a special interest. He or she seems to have been born with an attitude of dedication or ability to focus on his primary objective. There is unlimited patience while waiting for the exact expression to catch with a camera or the proper time to net that elusive butterfly.

Venus Vigintile Jupiter — From early childhood this native can weight decisions fairly and be diplomatic in giving a verdict. As the years pass he or she becomes more interested in seeing that justice is carried out in all matters in which he becomes involved. This aspect usually brings influence in the native's sphere of activity.

Venus Vigintile Saturn — This individual will attack cherished beliefs or institutions if he or she is convinced that they are perpetuating false impressions for the public. Seemingly aloof this person is actually quite perceptive.

They will be more apt to write of their opinions than voice them.

Venus Vigintile Uranus — Precocious in whatever field his or her interest lies this native must learn to live with unusual spurts of both physical and mental growth. When talents are developed too early they need to be balanced with expanding of other facets of life or trained into the proper channel so the energies are not burned out too soon.

Venus Vigintile Neptune — An author with this aspect can build characters from past acquaintances and experiences without any effort. Persons with this aspect in the natal horoscope are clever at doing impressions of others. They cross back and forth over the bridge between illusion and reality without disturbing their composure.

Venus Vigintile Pluto — A full realization of personal power and ability makes this individual less vulnerable to daily problems and annoyances. He or she can translate cosmic principles into poetry or invocations. They may be constantly cheering others with cute verses. This person walks with a distinctive stride and restores joy with vivid colors.

Vigintiles of Mars:

Mars Vigintile Ceres — This native enjoys working with the earth whether it be clay or pottery, farming, dyeing cloth with berries, or other such handicraft. Though pleasant appearing the individual is quite independent in thoughts and actions. There is also an interest in keeping the body fit through exercises, martial arts, yoga or hiking to mention a few ways.

Mars Vigintile Pallas Athena — Such a hard worker often goes into one of the professional sports fields to use this disciplined energy. The man or woman with this aspect in the natal horoscope usually has a very sturdy build, growing steadily over the years, unless this is strongly counterindicated elsewhere in the chart.

Mars Vigintile Juno — For some people the primary way to gain security is through marriage. So it is for this native who may wed more than once. He or she works with many people yet stands aloof from making friends with co-workers. There is an active curiosity which leads him or her to ask many questions in a courteous and dignified manner. This is a good aspect for a quiz show host or panel participant.

Mars Vigintile Vesta — This native goes ahead with his or her research regardless of how many people scoff at the basic theory or current findings. He likes to dig beneath the surface to find out what is really behind the legends or present philosophy. Deeply interested in the fundamental concepts of religion this person often does not participate in an orthodox ritualism throughout the whole of life but develops his or her own patterns of worship. This aspect brings things from the subconscious into the conscious awareness to be examined by analytical methods.

Mars Vigintile Jupiter — Although the person with this natal aspect has many friends and acquaintances he or she prefers doing a solo act in most cases. Having so many varied interests makes it difficult for other people to keep up with his or her activity. Always entertaining and interesting this native rarely lets another see his real inner thoughts or feelings.

Mars Vigintile Saturn — This individual is not so much concerned with the daily events and happenings as with the larger scope of activity in the world. He or she brings a respect of the past into any projects or jobs of the present.

Mars Vigintile Uranus — By working with what some people consider liabilities and turning them into assets people with this natal aspect win the respect and admiration of the world in general. Here is the ability to launch a great career from very little background and training.

Mars Vigintile Neptune — Having this combination of planets in the natal horoscope helps the native to be aware of the need for timing events properly. When the time is not right for acting it may be possible to set aside the plans and funds for that particular project to be handled more successfully later. This is the case with people who leave trust funds or endow foundations to make it possible for others to handle a special goal or dream.

Mars Vigintile Pluto — This well-coordinated person likes to work with groups, even to organizing new units of people. He or she knows how to handle situations where there are stronger people bullying weaker ones. He or she can put on a tough exterior for protection when needed.

Vigintiles of Jupiter:

Jupiter Vigintile Ceres — There is nothing this person enjoys as much as giving another a new start in life whether it be with career endeavors or family responsibilities. There is definitely a maternal feeling for all who come within his or her area. This is a good aspect for a pediatrician or obstetrician.

Jupiter Vigintile Pallas Athena — Sometimes a sidewalk-psychiatrist, at others a trained counselor, persons with this natal aspect like to help people understand themselves. This native works slowly up the ladder of success, having a measure of security along the way. He or she prefers to launch a career slowly, watching what is happening along the way.

Jupiter Vigintile Juno — These individuals enjoy presenting gifts or memorials in honor of loved ones. There is a fondness for ornate objects around the home usually to be more admired than used. In cases where the native was affiliated with an organized church he or she participated in preparing the altar for the various rituals.

Jupiter Vigintile Vesta — Even though this native may be called upon to make great sacrifices they will be done willingly. He or she understands the true meaning of valor. There is usually a dignity of stance and appearance with this natal aspect.

Jupiter Vigintile Saturn — This person prefers to be the absolute authority whether in a small group of friends, an enlarged family gathering or even on the world scene. He or she will fight for personal independence and will brook no attempt to stop his or her bid for freedom. When not thwarted this individual makes a good leader, being concerned for all who are placed in his care.

Jupiter Vigintile Uranus — A search for the meaning behind symbolism on all levels was found in the natives having this natal aspect. In some cases this was expressed by putting thoughts or old writings to music to give a sense of pattern to the whole. There was also found a great deal of emotional courage with this combination of planets.

Jupiter Vigintile Neptune — From world renown writers to local newspaper reporters, this particular combination of energies gives an insatiable curiosity to know about what is happening in the world. The native soars with his or her own imagination while rushing to share these impressions with anyone who will listen.

Jupiter Vigintile Pluto — If it is truly possible to become a legend in one's own time this native will achieve such an end. He or she sees the potential of new endeavors and puts energy into gaining favor and acceptance for such procedures. There is always an intensity of purpose no matter how small the scale upon which the individual is forced to work.

Vigintiles of Saturn, Uranus, Neptune and Pluto:

Because the slower moving planets create major and minor aspects only during certain years or periods the Vigintiles for Saturn, Uranus, Neptune and Pluto will be considered in their respective time frames. Persons born during various years react against the background of historical events as well as the natal horoscope.

Saturn Vigintile Uranus — When these planets are in approaching 18-degree angles with each other during the years 1940 and 1985 during this century there would be expected to be the culmination of new scientific research, a realignment of traditional and liberal thought, a return to some of the basic concepts of government and religion, as well as more of a balance between security and change. In 1940 the western nations were engaged in a major conflict, World War II, when every facet of life was undergoing stress and strain. Of course, there were other major and minor transiting aspects more responsible for the actual conflict than this one. Nevertheless, there was a definite return to the basic family structure and to traditional religious worship. What occurs in 1985 remains to be seen.

Saturn was moving away from Uranus in the separating Vigintile aspect during 1941 and 1942 as it will be again in 1991. For this country it meant that the entire nation was launched into a war which would begin a new cycle of change to last for decades.

Saturn Vigintile Neptune — The approaching aspects which have occurred were in 1915 plus 1951 and 1952 which upon first appearance have very little in common. However, these were periods when the medical profession was accepting new techniques which had been experimented with over periods of years. The practice of analyzing the subconscious became popular during both of these time periods. There was also an awareness of the problems of drug abuse during both of these time periods. The final such aspect of the century occurs in 1987.

When these two outer planets are separating Vigintile from each other in 1919, 1954 and again in 1991 it would be expected that the world would be experiencing some new beginnings in religion, medicine, subconscious behavior, underseas exploration, and other factors related to the planet being aspected. After World War I and the Korean War associated with the two former dates mentioned business and private industry came into these fields and began to use some of the technical experience which had been developed during the times of conflict.

Saturn Vigintile Pluto — From occurrences during the approaching Vigintile aspects in 1914 and 1946 we would expect similar effects in the year 1981. People born during both the earlier time periods have grown to maturity about the time of an economic world wide decline. Therefore, it has been up to these individuals to utilize the experiences of past decades to the best of their abilities to conserve available resources. This would appear that the potential for dealing with crisis was laid with the energies of these outer planets in the natal horoscopes of each generation.

When Saturn was separating from Pluto at the 18-degree aspect during 1916 and 1949 the world was engaged in actual conflict showing that changes were beginning which would completely revamp situations of power all over the world. This aspect repeats in 1983.

Uranus Vigintile Neptune — The only time when these two planets will be in the 18-degree of Vigintile aspect with each other is an applying aspect during the year 1984. Authors and playwrights have made this year famous as the time when the world will be under the control of "Big Brother."

Uranus Vigintile Pluto — An applying Vigintile of these two planets occurred in 1958 followed by a separating aspect in 1972. While there was a realigning of power between former enemies and allies one aspect is really not enough upon which to base future predictions. The separating aspect was shortly before the Watergate scandal which so disrupted the workings of the American executive office.

Neptune Vigintile Pluto — The single 18-degree aspect between these two farthest planets was happening during the early part of the century, around 1905 and 1906. As Neptune separated from Pluto the Twentieth Century was arriving with all of its changes in the lives of people upon this planet. Esoterically speaking it has been said that the planet Earth was then entering into another phase of its present initiation.

6

Semi-Octile Aspect

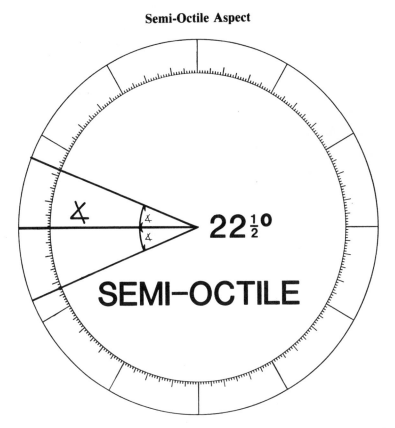

$22\frac{1}{2}°$

SEMI-OCTILE

This minor aspect has recently gained acceptance as a major cause of action among astrologers practicing the dial techniques of Cosmobiology and Uranian Astrology. The Semi-Octile or Semi-Semi-Square is one of the family of angles created by dividing the 360-degree circle by multiples of the number four. This particular arc of 22½ degrees is formed by dividing the circle by sixteen.

There is reason to believe that this aspect is particularly involved with health concerns which would certainly follow in the wake of excellent medical research done by Reinhold Ebertin and his associates.

No further research was done at the time of this writing to separate the effects of the Semi-Octile from other action aspects considered on the 45 or 90-degree dials. Sufficient to say that this aspect is being used more frequently as computers become widely used in calculating the smaller angles and will, in time, be given further keywords and understanding.

Glyph: ⊀

7

Quindecile Aspect

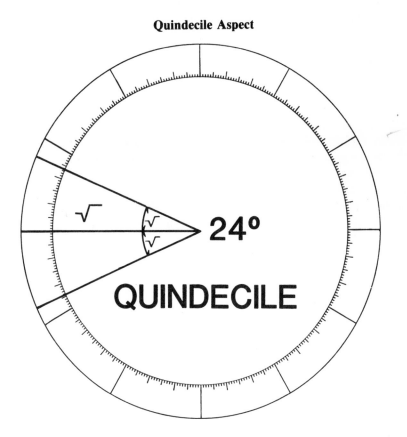

As planets reach 24 degrees in separating from the past conjunction with each other it is like the momentum as an automobile accelerates into the driving gear so that it can begin on the way to its destination. The few moments it takes for modern machines to reach this stage are less noticeable than when vehicles needed be shifted into higher gears as they gained momentum. Just so a 24-degree aspect, or Quindecile, of the fast moving Moon is much less obvious than the same aspect made by slow paced Saturn or Neptune.

When solar bodies are approaching each other at 24 degrees from conjunction there is the reaction of braking or slowing down the activity begun by the two energies involved. This is like lightly applying the brakes as a car approaches a caution light or stop sign preparatory to coming to a complete halt.

The Quindecile is formed by dividing the 360-degree circle into fifteen equal portions. An orb of only one degree is allowed for this aspect because of its close proximity to other minor aspects. There is not sufficient research to present delineations for all planets in Quindecile aspects to all others so only a few keywords are contined in this particular book.

Gylph: √
Keywords of the Quindecile:

acceleration
deceleration
braking

inspiration
momentum
surge

The following Esoteric interpretations of planets found in Quindecile aspect were given by Dr. Elisabeth V. Bacon of Columbus, Ohio:

When the double of twelve is considered it relates to inspiration as well as to organization. There were twelve elders of the Old Testament and twelve apostles of the New Testament. Man has 24 paracranial nerves, all related to the crowning. This means the person has accomplished and has been crowned by the Lord upon the Throne.

When the person is crowned, or has a 24-degree aspect to the following planet:

Moon — He has developed his psychic gifts and is powerful.

Sun — He has passed a very great initiation.

Mercury — He is crowned with mental faculties which will make him scientific or mentally aligned and logical.

Venus — He is crowned with the power of beauty.

Mars — He is crowned with energy, strength, direction and concentration.

Ceres — He is crowned with the ability to reap what he has worked for in other incarnations.

Jupiter — He is crowned with riches.

Saturn — He is crowned with a fatherly nature which can also be firm plus the ability to make true and right judgments.

Uranus — He will have the genius type mind or suffer from the karma of misusing brillance in a past life.

Neptune — He will understand the need for dissolving past dreams in order to make room for new ideals and visions.

Pluto — He will be good with gems, and can reach into the subconscious or other subterranean places.

8

Semi-Sextile Aspect

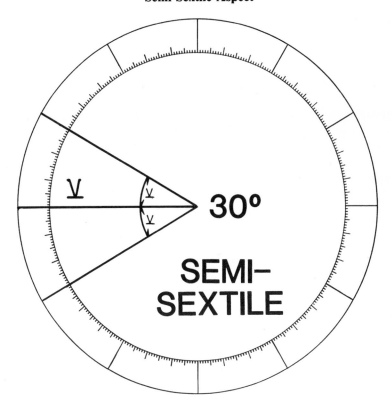

Although the Semi-Sextile aspect is usually dismissed as being a weak Sextile this minor angle or aspect has some distinction of its own. Being the product of division of the 360-degree circle into 12 equal segments the Semi-Sextile consists of a 30-degree angle measured within 1 or 2 degrees of orb.

The Semi-Sextile seems to be more inherited characteristics than actual opportunities. Sometimes these traits are beneficial while at other times they are handicaps which force the native to struggle through difficulties in order to succeed. At times the Semi-Sextile indicates the ability to capitalize on something begun by a parent or close relative.

In numerous instances the avocation became the primary means of livelihood after major changes or trials in life. Several times this was indicated by the Semi-Sextile when the native's favorite form of recreation was developed into a small, but successful, business venture after retirement.

With the Semi-Sextile benefits come from less apparent sources and are less tangible than with Sextile or Trine aspects. When the horoscope has a number of Semi-Sextiles throughout the various degrees of the circle it indicates a mixture of experiences because a variety of both Squares and Sextiles will be formed. This would also indicate a Locomotive Pattern, as explained by the late Marc Edmund Jones, which gives the tendency to react to stimuli with ceaseless activity until halted by yet another process.

Glyph: ⊻
Keywords of the Semi-Sextile:

assistance	cooperation	intangibles	possibilities
awareness	echoes	integration	practical
backstage	emergence	latent tendencies	supportive
boost	growth	management	thirst

Semi-Sextiles of the Sun:

Sun Semi-Sextile Moon — Gains and favors come from public figures for the native born with this aspect. It is good that opportunities abound for he is born with high aspirations. This aspect indicates being well-received by the public or having a special charm such as popular entertainers or actors have. There is also humanitarian compassion which makes the native work for charitable ventures.

Sun Semi-Sextile Mercury — Only a very wide version of this aspect would be possible in the natal horoscope because of the orbital patterns of Mercury around the Sun.

Sun Semi-Sextile Venus — A charming appearance with a well-formed body helps this native make the best of his or her good looks. There is a tendency to become chubby in later years so it is wise to watch the food intake. Luxuries are possible either through his or her own efforts or through the achievements of relatives. This native is a welcome guest at a party or home because of an infectious sense of humor which may be shown as practical jokes.

Sun Semi-Sextile Mars — Cheerfulness and enthusiasm are contagious which adds to this native's chances for success. Being a hard worker he or she is also pleasant about fulfilling even the meanest tasks. There is determination to proceed through set-backs or difficulties.

Sun Semi-Sextile Ceres — A youthful appearance makes people want to mother these natives. Where there is a choice he or she will receive the benefit of the doubt. Many persons having this aspect were born into talented families who had the knowledge of proper methods of training their nature abilities. In some cases, the mother or father was more a coach than parent by treatment and attitude.

Sun Semi-Sextile Pallas Athena — There is a certain insight about time for sharing wisdom, possessions, experience, beauty or sorrow, burdens or happiness as well as any property. Persons having this angular relationship in their natal horoscopes have an understanding of the true meaning of transaction; they understand how to exchange things of a certain value for items of similar importance.

Sun Semi-Sextile Juno — Where this aspect was found there was the ability to integrate personal problems or experiences into character portrayals whether on stage or in writings. Brilliant performances need not, however, promise happiness in intimate relationships. Being a perfectionist often leads to physical strain.

Sun Semi-Sextile Vesta — The monastic life style is sought by persons having this natal aspect. Through discipline they are able to dispense with much of what the world considers necessities. He or she finds fulfillment in the simple life style.

Sun Semi-Sextile Jupiter — The ultimate victory belongs to these natives. Becoming famous by virtue of their own hard work and skills they eventually win out over all others. This aspect is strong in the horoscopes of important persons who are lauded for their efforts. They usually have money for desired investments.

Sun Semi-Sextile Saturn — In many fields it is important to have a good sense of timing. This aspect indicates that ability as well as the capacity to learn from past experiences. Even though these people back the underdog in most situations they are proud of their own heritage. Being well paced wins more races than jumping out of the starting gate ahead of the other contestants.

Sun Semi-Sextile Uranus — Those who celebrate the successes of others show a great deal of self confidence. These natives are as innovative in their support of others as they would be in personal competition. Several persons having this aspect provided the sound track, or voice, for another person's performance. This aspect also was present in the horoscopes of cartoonists and puppetteers.

Sun Semi-Sextile Neptune — By and large these natives are sensitive persons with the ability to personify an idea or an image. They research their hunches thoroughly. Though not always beautiful or handsome, they have a glamour which comes across well through the medium of the camera.

Sun Semi-Sextile Pluto — Whether these people receive credit for unusual achievements or win acclaim for bringing hidden treasures to light they seem almost guided by mystical forces. In some cases he or she interpreted great truths for the masses, in others the native led a compatible group of volunteers, while yet again this aspect prompted a person to be extremely interested in problems of ecology. There is a desire to conserve resources by recycling them again and again.

Semi-Sextiles of the Moon:

Moon Semi-Sextile Mercury — Practical ideas pour forth with little effort for these natives. Whether successful comic, media star or popular writer they appeal to young audiences as well as mature viewers and readers. This aspect gives one the ability to be persistent in study efforts as well as the capability to speak extemporaneously about a variety of subjects.

Moon Semi-Sextile Venus — Being surrounded by supportive friends makes it easier to be optimistic. Even though this native is naturally graceful it is helpful to cultivate additional charms. Learning to be moderate about expressing opinions brings eventual approval.

Moon Semi-Sextile Mars — Regardless of being born with a lot of physical stamina these natives always draw assistance to them when they are completing chores. A well coordinated body makes it easy to excel at any chosen sport. He or she loves to shop for bargains and purchase things on sale.

Moon Semi-Sextile Ceres — Basically uncomplicated, a person having this aspect is quite interested in home and family. He or she will be a concerned parent who continues to share the joys and sorrows of children's lives far into adulthood. Some of this native's fondest memories stem from family holidays or traditions.

Moon Semi-Sextile Pallas Athena — Desire for a successful career is a motivating factor throughout life for this native. For a woman this is enhanced by having parents who were able to exchange roles without losing their basic femininity or masculinity. There is mathematical understanding.

Moon Semi-Sextile Juno — A thirst for acclaim leads these natives to develop a particular public charm. Often they have mates who assist them in expanding an enjoyable recreation into a life commitment. He or she can be quite ridiculous and yet remain believable, which is a necessary ingredient in creating good comedy.

Moon Semi-Sextile Vesta — Emotions are always near the surface for persons born with these two solar bodies in aspect. An actor or actress having this aspect can fully express his or her own interpretation of a given role.

Moon Semi-Sextile Jupiter — Such a sympathetic individual is gracious even when making requests. A native having this aspect usually has a very positive outlook which improves most situations. Being innovative insures that career preferences will be heeded when dealing with the creative arts.

Moon Semi-Sextile Saturn — Persons having this particular aspect in the natal horoscope tend to abide by their own consciences. They look over a situation carefully and then make decisions accordingly.

Moon Semi-Sextile Uranus — Family support is necessary in helping these natives achieve their greatest desires. This person relates well to symbolism whether it be mathematics or mythology. He or she usually is oriented toward the future, not the past, and so is able to put past mistakes or injuries aside while planning and working for upcoming events. In some cases natives having this aspect were able to stage unusual comebacks from debilitating situations.

Moon Semi-Sextile Neptune — The great idealist who is always searching for answers intuitively knows that true value lies beyond the material. A person having this aspect has empathy with others which may be used in developing characters in a novel, winning the jury to a client's testimony, or simply in working with friends.

Moon Semi-Sextile Pluto — This person is unafraid to question the highest authority for correct answers even though he or she values an expert opinion from any professional. Such a person will also plan to have some time alone throughout the day. He or she looks for the good qualities in acquaintances and friends.

Semi-Sextiles of Mercury:

Mercury Semi-Sextile Venus — Friendliness, such as this native has, is the best asset of a really good salesman. Audiences are friendly and responsive to a person who gives much of him or herself. Usually people having this aspect are born of a good family heritage.

Mercury Semi-Sextile Mars — Logic goes hand in hand with the bountiful energy to carry out obligations. Great opportunities arise periodically for persons with this aspect. It is wise to take immediate advantage of such chances for they are not long lasting.

Mercury Semi-Sextile Ceres — This is a good aspect for a teacher of small children who must put theory into practical usage. It also shows understanding and compassion for the sick and elderly. This native can "make do" with the tools at hand.

Mercury Semi-Sextile Pallas Athena — When this aspect is present in the natal horoscope there is the tendency to work within a family business or endeavor. Sometimes the native is involved with brothers and sisters, in other instances his or her own children seek employment in the same profession as their parent. Astute business sense is present.

Mercury Semi-Sextile Juno — Natives with this combination of solar bodies often have a friendly rapport with their mates which leads to teamwork whether it be in parenting, remodeling the house or even in joint business ventures. They find a purpose in working within groups or partnership situations.

Mercury Semi-Sextile Vesta — Finding someone or something to protect and care for is a motivating factor for an individual with this particular aspect. He or she feels most beneficial to society when placed in the role of defender or guardian.

Mercury Semi-Sextile Jupiter — Many prolific writers have this combination of planets in their natal horoscopes. Even people who have not been published tend to keep voluminous journals or diaries. It is also a good aspect for an inventor or designer because it gives an agile mind.

Mercury Semi-Sextile Saturn — Skilled debators, qualified statesmen and renown educators have this minor aspect in common. An individual having this angle learns the art of compromise at an early age. He or she also tends to believe that tried and true methods serve well until new techniques are fully developed. This native normally has a very rational thought process.

Mercury Semi-Sextile Uranus — Surprising news comes through unexpected channels for these natives. They are quite often nimble footed and dexterous. Productive, original minds utilize simple information to develop new concepts. Though visionaries they are usually cooperative with friends and co-workers.

Mercury Semi-Sextile Neptune — Honesty is appealing for these persons who enjoy probing beyond the obvious. This is a good aspect for an amateur sleuth or a professional detective. Persons having this aspect varied greatly in their choice of professions but all shared the desire to look behind the evident, or "lift the veils." Some were even obsessed with exploring various ideas about death.

Mercury Semi-Sextile Pluto — A quaint drawl or friendly smile appeals to the public more than practiced mannerisms. Natives with this aspect eventually find that there is satisfaction in the little pleasures of life as well as great accomplishments. They have a tendency to search astutely, to investigate ideas in depth and to look at time as the great validator of unusual theories. People having this aspect often work with the handicapped in one way or another.

Semi-Sextiles of Venus:

Venus Semi-Sextile Mars — In every case investigated natives having this aspect were born into a harmonious family situation. Although this does not necessarily indicate monetary wealth there was the security of being cherished and accepted. These people have a sense of gratification from early childhood. Being accepted as an individual gives the confidence to explore fields of interest whether it be charting new lands or introducing fresh lyrics.

Venus Semi-Sextile Ceres — Training in specific disciplines during early childhood guides these natives in later positions of leadership. Often he or she interits a position bringing honor and respect. In a few instances this aspect was present when the native was literally worshipped by his followers. This is definitely one of the minor indicators of early, though not lasting, popularity.

Venus Semi-Sextile Pallas Athena — Career endeavors are associated with an appreciation of harmony and beauty when people have this aspect prominent in the horoscope. Artists, photographers and decorators are among the natives reacting to this combination of planetary energies.

Venus Semi-Sextile Juno — There is a love and respect for pomp and ceremony with this particular stellar angle. Fleeting fame waits at the end of many years of diligent adherence to the rules of one's order or profession. Family members openly show their appreciation for long periods of service and fidelity. Often he or she is appointed to be the spokesman for relatives or co-workers.

Venus Semi-Sextile Vesta — Being generous, artistic and capable this native must publicly laugh in the face of personal heartbreak. There is often estrangement from loved ones so it is well that he or she adapts easily to being alone. This person enjoys doing favors for other people.

Venus Semi-Sextile Jupiter — Coming from a secure family background is a good aspect for any person aspiring to be a writer, artist, actor or actress, or any of the other creative professions. This combination brings a sense of color blending or musical harmony. For the native there is an unexplained knowledge of "his or her own place in the world."

Venus Semi-Sextile Saturn — Faithful actions are appreciated and reciprocated by family and friends. This native learns to look to his or her elders for affection and advice. While not overly demonstrative the individual likes to be generous with gifts and raises.

Venus Semi-Sextile Uranus — Latent talents have been known to develop after tragedy or shock. When this occurs the rewards are doubly prized. This aspect gives the courage and ability to snap back after hardships. The type of encouragement which innovates comes from loved ones and acquaintances. Receiving unexpected favors becomes common for natives having this aspect.

Venus Semi-Sextile Neptune — When these two bodies are separated by the 30-degree angle the native learns to turn handicaps into advantages. Through this lesson great strides and gains are made. He or she is quite sympathetic and may even marry a disadvantaged person.

Venus Semi-Sextile Pluto — Public recognition brings the fulfillment of hopes and wishes for this native. He or she learns to accept the many gifts coming his way. This is a good person to invite to a party or choose for member of a team.

Semi-Sextiles of Mars:

Mars Semi-Sextile Ceres — Persons born with this combination of planetary energies tend to work with elemental substances like clay and pastel crayons. They capitalize on their simple upbringings and use common sense in their drive for importance.

Mars Semi-Sextile Pallas Athena — This native is a hard worker who enjoys being in constant demand. He or she is never so happy as when being needed. There are latent tendencies to succeed, in career endeavors, against tremendous odds. Emerging on top in a competition is not as unusual as the fact that these people also receive heart-felt best wishes from their challengers and opponents.

Mars Semi-Sextile Juno — A quick temper mars otherwise happy relationships for this person. He or she is usually quite appealing to the opposite sex and has no trouble developing new partnerships when the old ones break apart.

Mars Semi-Sextile Vesta — Caution is the keyword for an individual having this aspect in the natal horoscope. The only danger is of becoming overly timid and withdrawn.

Mars Semi-Sextile Jupiter — When this individual has the finances he or she will decorate the home and surroundings lavishly. If funds are sparse he or she will make up by being clever and inventive. Many of these persons either volunteer to work for charitable organizations or solicit money for worthwhile projects. They have a sense of humor which enjoys puns and jokes as well as liking to have people around all the time. This is a good aspect for a night-club entertainer or comedian. It is a useful trait for professional military officers.

Mars Semi-Sextile Saturn — This is a person who gets down to business quickly and cheerfully. He or she makes a good co-worker as he can be harnassed into teamwork situations. Security comes from being able to make long range plans.

Mars Semi-Sextile Uranus — Innovative techniques work best for these individuals. With this natal aspect the person looks for unusual settlements for arguments or problems. He or she is well organized and takes charge in a crisis situation.

Mars Semi-Sextile Neptune — With the ability to be more psychic or intuitive than normal this person must be aware of the problems of becoming involved in unusual religions or movements. By learning to consider the ramifications before taking action he or she can use this inherited ability to an advantage.

Mars Semi-Sextile Pluto — In an emergency it is helpful to have these persons who are good at repairing malfunctioning machinery. Listening to his or her own impressions makes this native a good explorer or scientist. There may also be an interest in salvaging sunken treasure, traveling into unexplored areas of the world, or simply participating in games of chance.

Semi-Sextiles of Jupiter:

Jupiter Semi-Sextile Ceres — By and large these natives develop their natural coordination and abilities to super stardom. Where there is a great deal of natural talent it usually surfaces early in life. With this aspect there will be relatives or parents around who see that this ability is channeled, trained and used.

Jupiter Semi-Sextile Pallas Athena — A philosophic mind combined with quick wit makes this person popular with either friends or an audience. However, they prefer to refrain from making their personal lives and views common knowledge. He or she is an amiable person to be around. Never underestimate this person's shrewdness in business dealings.

Jupiter Semi-Sextile Juno — Being able to sublimate personal desires completely is an aid to success for this person but can bring havoc to private relationships. Usually, the husband or wife is helpful in promoting the native. As an actor or actress he can lose himself so fully in a role as to create magnificent characters or images.

Jupiter Semi-Sextile Vesta — There is great dedication of purpose with this combination of planets in the natal horoscope. The native has a sustaining religious faith even though he or she expresses no orthodox views.

Jupiter Semi-Sextile Saturn — Even when there is no training in business methods this native falls into positions of leadership either by inheriting a company, by assisting a friend, or by being appointed to a political office. This person is capable of sustained effort over a long period of time without losing his or her efficiency. He or she is placed in power because of this natural discipline and executive ability. These traits can just as easily be manifested in volunteer organizations as in managerial placements.

Jupiter Semi-Sextile Uranus — In many cases a native having this natal aspect suddenly moved from his or her homeland into a completely foreign situation. Because of such a drastic change he was led to explore unknown traditions or concepts. Assistance is always available.

Jupiter Semi-Sextile Neptune — A strong religious upbringing gives this native the background to face future endeavors with faith and tranquility. In several cases the native integrated personal spiritual development into writing or publishing of religious or occult books. Intuitive ability comes naturally and gives the individual insight into methods of approach to people and situations.

Jupiter Semi-Sextile Pluto — Several persons having this natal aspect were founders of large movements or organizations. The native either inherits wealth and glory or receives his or her fondest wish without undue effort. A powerful inner attraction is present without cultivation or practice.

Semi-Sextiles of Saturn, Uranus, Neptune and Pluto:

Because the slower moving planets create major and minor aspects only during certain years or periods the Semi-Sextiles for Saturn, Uranus, Neptune and Pluto will be considered in their respective time frames. Persons born during various years react against the background of historical events.

Saturn Semi-Sextile Uranus — At the turn of the century Saturn was making one of three separating Semi-Sextiles during this hundred year period when the world was emerging into a new economic and social structure. Other separating Semi-Sextiles are during the last years of World War II as new alliances and boundaries were being drawn up, and during the opening years of the last decade of the Twentieth Century when there may again emerge new ways of accomodating the teeming masses of humanity now present.

The only approaching Semi-Sextile between Saturn and Uranus which history can detail was in the late 1930's when this planet was recovering from a severe depression and heading into world-wide conflict. This aspect is repeated in 1983 and 1984 with hopefully different results.

Saturn Semi-Sextile Neptune — The approaching Semi-Sextiles of Saturn to Neptune were in 1914 and 1950 when there were conflicts in the Eastern Hemisphere which also affected Western countries. Many of the social codes changed because of world conditions and, in each case, there was an upsurge of religious revivals and ecumenical movements. When this aspect is repeated during 1985 and 1986 it is hoped that major religions will again be able to highlight their common heritage rather than their ritualistic and doctrinal differences.

As Saturn separated from Neptune at 30 degrees during 1920 and 1956 America was concerned first with laws prohibiting use of alcohol and, secondly, with the increased shipment of drugs into this country from Asia and Middle East. Both were periods following conflicts which necessitated shipping American servicemen into different cultures where they both learned something of other traditions and intermarried with women from other races. So, to a degree, Neptune was being activated to dissolve barriers of time and space which exist between nations. The next separating Semi-Sextile between Saturn and Neptune will be in 1992.

Saturn Semi-Sextile Pluto — Saturn was 30 degrees from a Conjunction with Pluto during the 1912-1913 period and again in 1945. Governments were realigning themselves to achieve greater power at the same time that national interests were being strengthened. It was a time when mankind began to feel more secure than in previous periods. People born during these two times have an inner sense of security, of knowing exactly who they are, more than most other persons born during this century. The next such aspect between these two planets occurred last year and will take some time to evaluate as these natives grow to maturity. It is almost like the lull which occurs in the eye of a tornado or hurricane, a false sense of peace and security.

In looking at the separating Semi-Sextiles between Saturn and Pluto there were obviously the tensions of world conflict during 1917 and 1950. The next such aspect will be effective during the years of 1984 to 1986 when many science fiction authors and economists have suggested major lifestyle changes for the entire globe.

Uranus Semi-Sextile Neptune — The only time when these two heavy planets were 30 degrees apart during the Twentieth Century was during the years between 1976 and 1979 with Uranus approaching a Conjunction with Neptune around 1993 and 1994. This can presently be seen as an integration of ideals forced upon mankind by present difficulties and shortages. How it will affect children born during those years remains to be seen. Hopefully there will be an outgrowth of humanitarian principles and activity leading into the coming Aquarian Age. Certainly there has been a wealth of metaphysical and occult material loosed upon the world in the form of books, classes, media presentations and lectures so that the organized religious community has been forced to consider the validity of some less conventional theories and practices.

Uranus Semi-Sextile Pluto — Uranus both approached and separated from Pluto at the Semi-Sextile aspect during the middle of this century. The approaching aspect during 1953 and 1954 saw the integration of long standing theories and brought some ancient concepts into manifestation. Metaphysical theories proposed for hundreds of years were finally proved by scientific discoveries. Further investigation into nuclear fission shocked the research community to look into the past as well as the future for answers. Space flights were becoming more possible with the development of new fuels and alloys. The science fiction stories of the past were being integrated into reality of the present and future.

The separating aspect occurred in the late 1970's as the world was emerging into some new alignments. Problems of overpopulation, food and fuel shortages, land depletion, economic inflation, and chemical waste were among the many demanding immediate solution from government leaders. Even the crust of the earth was reacting with a record number of tornadoes and hurricanes, volcanic eruptions, forest fires and droughts.

Neptune Semi-Sextile Pluto — The only period when these two outer bodies were 30 degrees apart was during World War I as Neptune was pulling ahead of Pluto along the Zodiacal path. Strong leaders for future generations were born during that time of tumult when Pluto was exhibiting its then unknown effect of disrupting the status quo. The old order of European royalty was being dissolved and replaced by more democratic forms of government. Women were struggling for their rights alongside men. The Russian serfs had risen up against the centuries long domination of a Tsar and his family. China was beginning its long battle against the established monarchy. India and Africa were beginning to rebel against European domination. Even in the Western Hemisphere the small provinces and islands were pulling away from their former owners and heading toward eventual affiliation with the Americas. So this could truly be seen as the emerging of the dissolution of old powers to be replaced eventually by new authorities. It was also a time of illusion and idealism when man felt that armed conflict might be over permanently. World War I was often called the "war to end all wars."

9

Decile Aspect

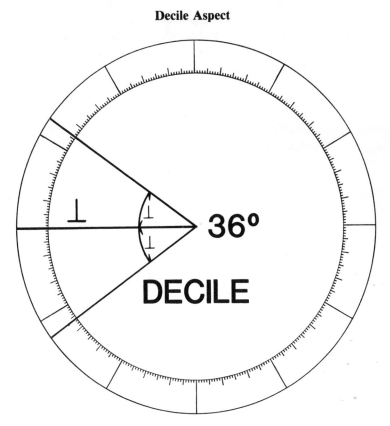

As the number Ten represents Perfected Man or new beginnings on a higher level of the spiral of life in the study of Numerology aspects derived by dividing the 360-degree circle by ten would be expected to have some of those characteristics. The Decile, or 36-degree angle, is also half of a Quintile aspect and so is related to that family of aspects.

In Homeopathic Medicine the theory is to dilute the dosage of medicine thus making it more potent. According to that practice a solution containing one-thousandth of a serum or chemical element is stronger than one containing one-hundredth or one-tenth. The principle is that when you dilute the original an illusion of the remedy remains which reacts on the subtle bodies of the individual rather than on the physical entity. Allergy specialists use this concept in giving the patient minute doses of the substance to which the patient reacts until his or her body builds up a natural barrier to the offending material.

Thus, as expected, the Decile aspect reacts in subtle ways rather than as obvious activity. This aspect may be found in the chart of the teacher who supports and develops the talents of students in her realm of influence rather than uses natural abilities to promote her own position in life. It is indicative of those who would develop groups to carry out new potentials for this aspect shows a true enjoyment of people. Natives having a Decile aspect between two planets will be able to understand and use the subtle essences of those planets in a very practical manner. This aspect indicates the practical usage of the talents involved, like using a moderate artistic ability in handicrafts or amateur theater stage designs.

There is not sufficient research to present delineations for all the planets in Decile aspect to all others so these few keywords will be all that is contained in this particular book. An orb of 1 to 2 degrees is usually given for this aspect.

Glyph: ⊥

Keywords of the Decile:

assembles	insight	polishes	shapes
calming	intuitive	practical	sociable
compassionate	mentor	resourceful	supportive
crafts	organized	scientific	utilizes

10

Novile Aspect

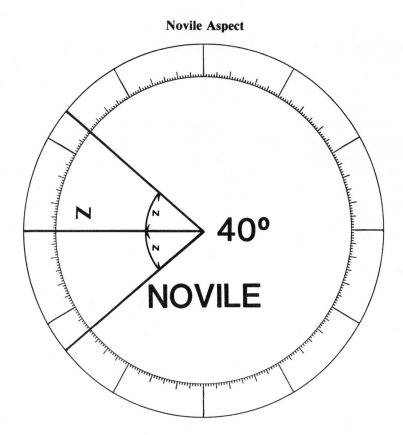

40°

NOVILE

Brooding is a good new keyword for the 40-degree aspect, termed Novile by Hindu astrologers and called the Nonagon by Western astrologers. It fits the concept as part of the Ninth Harmonic; that is, division of the 360-degree circle by the number nine.

A period of gestation, completion of programmed or planned activity such as describes the hen who sets upon her nest warming the eggs thereby assuring proper conditions for hatching of the baby chickens. Some hens are more temperamentally suited to this patience-instilling task than others so they may well be called upon to hatch the eggs of another fowl; as man is often requested to brood upon, or bring to fruition, the nebulous creative sparks of another human being.

The brooding or setting hen needs peace, subdued light and quiet to complete her task. There is also a softening of the underbreast which biologically could suggest calcium deficiencies.

From *The Center of the Cyclone* Dr. Lilly says, "Pupation can create a butterfly or a monster." During the process there is a gathering and a consolidating motion much like the billows of an accordian while being played.

In Indian astrology this aspect is considered to indicate the fertility of the couple involved. Because producing offspring is an important factor determining success or failure of union in that Eastern country the 40-degree aspect has long been used by Hindu astrologers when delineating compatibility. The Sidereal technique is more accurately termed the Novien Chart or Ninth Harmonic. Completion of creative endeavors shows by this aspect.

Esoterically the Novile indicates relationships between different planes of existence sometimes called parallel worlds. The 40-degree angle may well indicate "gates" between these dimensions for the particular individual.

An orb of 1 to 2 degrees is usually given when considering the Novile aspect in the natal horoscope.

Glyph: **N**

Keywords of the Novile:

birth	development	growth	release
brooding	devotion	nourishment	productive
completion	fertility	nurturing	supportive
creative	gestation	refines	testing

Myrna Lofthus, in her book *A Spiritual Approach to Astrology,* suggests that the karmic meaning of the 40-degree aspect is restriction created from past life situations. Esoteric Novile relationships between various planets are given in detail in this comprehensive Lofthus text.

Noviles of the Sun:

Sun Novile Moon — This aspect is esoterically called the physical incarnation of the Divine Ego. On a more practical level it gives an analytical attitude which shows concern with what is about to occur. This is neither fear nor joy but being deliberate in emotions and reactions. By selecting goals to reach and methods of activity before taking steps in any direction the native has fewer aftereffects on either the physical or the emotional plane.

Sun Novile Mercury — This aspect is not possible in the natal horoscope because of the orbital patterns of Mercury around the Sun.

Sun Novile Venus — Entertaining by nature, an individual with these planets in 40 degrees of each other likes to nurture creativity in artistic people. They often make it possible for children to advance in life. There is concern with refining the diet to get the best possible nutrition. It is a fertile aspect, especially in a woman's chart. He or she incubates ideas for offspring to carry out in later years.

Sun Novile Mars — When this competent leader masters his or her sexual struggles he can channel these energies into constructive efforts. One such person became known as the leader of "non-violent demonstrations" throughout the world. Through this aspect the proper balance to success is forced and obtained.

Sun Novile Ceres — This blending of planetary energies shows the mother who conscientiously keeps both her body and mind happy, clean and healthy during pregnancy for the benefit of the unborn child. Or this 40-degree angle equally denotes the student or businessman who approaches a next task or test with courage and controlled optimism.

Sun Novile Pallas Athena — One of the most positive aspects for a good teacher or professor this angle shows concern for the development of his or her students. There is also an understanding that teaching, whether formal or informal, enriches the teacher more than the student. An individual having this natal combination of planets thinks and speaks deliberately.

Sun Novile Juno — Several natives having this aspect spent their lives nurturing the bond between man and animals. In other cases this bond was between people of different cultures. There is a need to blend, whether it be ingredients in a recipe or concepts and ideas. In every case these natives were brillant strategists who handle interviews and confrontations with diplomacy. They tend to be attractive physically, even to the point of being quite handsome.

Sun Novile Vesta — A person born with this aspect in the natal horoscope prefers to spend time alone as much as possible. They need time for solitude and study. Sometimes these people become self-styled reformers when they re-enter the world of business and relationships.

Sun Novile Jupiter — Scientific researchers born with this natal aspect find support in the most unexpected places. Grants and fellowships become available to aid in continuation of their work. Letters and words of encouragement come from family and employers alike.

Sun Novile Saturn — Being protective of parents and elderly persons in general is one manifestation of this aspect. Another shows need to be very careful about breaking of bones because they take extra time to heal. There is often a role reversal in later life, when father becomes son to the offspring.

Sun Novile Uranus — This individual releases exciting or startling new information to small groups of friends or students. He or she is involved with philosophical approaches which grows out of contacts with other planes of existence. Sometimes this leads to the birth of a new theosophy or philosophy, at other times the information remains secluded with immediate associates.

Sun Novile Neptune — Besides exhibiting evangelistic fervor about religious subjects this native is usually clairvoyant, to one degree or another depending upon whether the ability is developed. Telepathic contact comes easily for him. He or she is interested in life after death and other related theories. It is important that creative energies be used in a constructive way and not wrongly directed.

Sun Novile Pluto — Working with groups is significant for individuals having this aspect in their natal horoscopes. They have charisma to develop leadership potentials shown elsewhere in the personality. This aspect gives the patience necessary for completing tasks begun out of enthusiasm for a cause or movement.

Noviles of the Moon:

Moon Novile Mercury — Whether they have biological children or merely care for other people's offspring these natives train children to follow their lead. The parental instincts are strong. He or she may be rather prudish or strict in manner of speech. Nevertheless, they are accomplished at speaking in public places or at professional gatherings.

Moon Novile Venus — There is the ability to heal long-standing emotional wounds with great compassion when a person has this natal aspect. They reflect upon the past to determine proper action to take in the present. While this attitude may seem submissive and non-assertive it is simply one of true humility.

Moon Novile Mars — Because this native is thrilled by dangerous situations he or she is constantly creating new diversions for excitement. There is a sense of intrigue about these individuals.

Moon Novile Ceres — Children with this natal aspect grow in ability and understanding beyond the mother's fondest wishes. There is an aptitude to harmonize with the forces of nature. It is almost as if they listen to the voice of the wind blowing about them. These people are quite receptive.

Moon Novile Pallas Athena — Even though persons with this natal aspect usually need to work hard throughout most of their lives they are cheerful about job conditions. Such an individual may be described as practical or down to earth. They attain leadership through following guidance that comes from co-workers and employees.

Moon Novile Juno ⌐ When this individual can refrain from negative thoughts and words he or she can make use of the gentle nature beneath a gruff exterior. This aspect gives the ability to blend the aggressive and receptive parts of the personality into a balance of forces. It is an energy that teaches patience.

Moon Novile Vesta — During the life there will be a time to rebuild both family and career because of conditions forced upon the native. Often there is need to flee restrictions or confinement whether from parental sternness or political purges. This combination of energies gives the native the courage to push emotional trauma aside and build on future hopes and opportunities.

Moon Novile Jupiter — Surprisingly this aspect denotes being in the public eye during childhood and youth. It can indicate being one of the individuals in a multiple birth or having many offspring. This native compensates for deficiencies with determined effort. He or she is strong minded or opinionated, but not to the degree of being obnoxious.

Moon Novile Saturn — By reviewing and analyzing the familiar it is possible for a native with this aspect to develop new forms out of the old. They work well with colors, often diversifying traditional pigments into new hues and tones. There can be the blending of two mediums to develop an entirely new expression. He or she needs time alone to develop and channel feelings into concrete form.

Moon Novile Uranus — An ability to adjust to outward changes may make this individual seem unfeeling or insensitive. Quite the opposite is true since they learn early in life to control emotional outbursts. They adjust to endurable situations because to resist only invites more problems or disaster. A good person to have around in times of stress or emergency.

Moon Novile Neptune — Not being afraid of death is an asset when working in the medical professions or following a military career. But the same characteristic may be a detriment to an entertainer or test pilot. There is the tendency to take chances beyond the realm of practical action with this natal aspect. The discreet use of power brings success but this native needs to learn not to overstep the bounds of human strength and agility.

Moon Novile Pluto — Even a physical deformity or disability does not keep people from liking this native. Limitations only helps these individuals evolve into wiser and more capable persons. Such leaders can demonstrate the productivity of limitation whether to a small group of followers or to a whole nation.

Noviles of Mercury:

Mercury Novile Venus — An individual having this natal aspect enjoys writing in a secluded country retreat. He or she builds a home or nest wherever he happens to be at the moment. They promote causes by writing about the subject in question. It is very easy to generate sympathy for a personal point of view. These planetary energies make it possible for the native to open earthly lines of communication, thus becoming a link between peoples and helping them to communicate more freely.

Mercury Novile Mars — Being a bold, dramatic crusader is easy for such an outspoken person. Although he or she is well liked, he values personal freedom and privacy above all. This native develops his eccentricities and allow them to become embellished to the point of becoming somewhat of a legend.

Mercury Novile Ceres — Interest in various methods of healing are present in this native. He or she may investigate approaches from reflexology to flower remedies, from Oriental accupressure to folk medicine, or from diets to rolfing. Sometimes they write about such experiences in order to promote their own findings or opinions. This disarming native has graceful hand movements which express well in playing the piano, dancing the traditional hula, drawing illustrations or other such skills. There is always present the desire to explore human nature in relation to the present environment.

Mercury Novile Pallas Athena — By examining the past the creative powers of the future are revealed. So it is with the native having this aspect in his or her horoscope who becomes interested in geneology. Keeping notes about a family tree or preparing notebooks and journals about such activity is of interest to this person. There is also the practical wisdom to understand when activity is futile and when it is beneficial.

Mercury Novile Juno — Realizing that it is ridiculous to become angry about minor faults of others makes it easier for this native to become involved in relationships with family and friends. There is the wisdom to restrain displays of temper or to hesitate uttering rash words. Some nervous tension is present which may be controlled by setting aside times to be alone or in peaceful surroundings.

Mercury Novile Vesta — This native goes back to old myths or traditions to investigate their authenticity and meaning for today's world. He or she often is a tireless writer and lecturer about such problems as ecology, endangered species, population control, chemical wastes, or other such humanitarian concerns. In addition, there is the tendency to spend long hours trying to learn to communicate with other species of animals. There is always an urge to explore unusual new concepts with the purpose of revealing more of the Divine Plan to mankind. Writings are inclined to be motivated by the idea of guidance from another plane of existence.

Mercury Novile Jupiter — A prolific writer, whether published or not, this native enjoys simplifying information from great theological or philosophical tenants. A good aspect for one who helps write condensed books or reviews of popular publications. There is an interest in religion. This individual can also be a writer of ballads or folk songs.

Mercury Novile Saturn — Such a talented speaker usually needs little or no training to become a public drawing card whether on the lecture circuit, the professional or amateur stage, the pulpit or any such position. Hardworking, ambitious and capable this native will achieve whatever he or she decides to attempt.

Mercury Novile Uranus — Development of unique speech patterns was the only thing natives having this aspect had in common. From brilliant comedians through award winning actors and public officials to a limited number of autistic children there was an unusual way of expressing oneself when people had this aspect in the natal horoscope. There seemed to be a strong desire to be individualistic.

Mercury Novile Neptune — There is a natural talent which can be developed into writing poetry. This native is quite a dreamer, even to being oblivious to threat of scandal perpetuated by personal activity.

Mercury Novile Pluto — When these natives assume the position of teachers they try to instill and nurture great cosmic truths in the minds of their students. They voice ideas of upheavals to come as well as relate those of the past. These individuals encourage pupils to rebel and expand their horizons. He or she tries to remove barriers between people and cultures.

Noviles of Venus:

Venus Novile Mars — Having a good physical body this individual enjoys being in the outdoors. He or she finds it exciting to develop old tales of courage and bravery of frontiersmen into interesting characters and stories which audiences enjoy hearing. There is a boldness which comes from self confidence.

Venus Novile Ceres — A wise man or woman cares for his or her own needs and the nourishment of friends and family simultaneously. This results in a fulfilled and placid attitude toward life. An individual having this natal aspect is self reliant.

Venus Novile Pallas Athena — There is the ability to develop an inherited talent into professional excellence for this native. Musical aptitude is usually present. He or she passes initial tests with flying colors born of the assurance of a combination of talent and hard work.

Venus Novile Juno — An insistence that the letter of the law be carried out can result in this native having money tied up in litigation sometime during the life. Nevertheless, there is the determination to make some of the dreams of childhood come true. He or she customarily dresses in a stylish and attractive manner.

Venus Novile Vesta — Virtue and responsibility prevail with this aspect. Here is the friend who will complete the task begun and abandoned by a more venturesome associate. Being around this native is like sitting beside a peaceful river. He or she will remain loyal and modest.

Venus Novile Jupiter — After a long search great wealth may be uncovered by an individual having this natal aspect. He or she will share and share alike with associates. In some cases, this bounty is in the form of wisdom, not material goods. Life is like a marathon to this person who enjoys the race as much as the reward.

Venus Novile Saturn — Courts protect the property and fortune of persons having this aspect in the natal horoscope. Just rewards are delivered after due time has elapsed, whether monetary or honorary. This native is a conscientious teacher or professor who develops class lectures on profound knowledge.

Venus Novile Uranus — This individual enjoys the thrill of contests and games of chance. Many persons having this natal aspect were military officers with a reputation of being excellent strategists.

Venus Novile Neptune — Intense and imaginative, this native makes a good appearance on either stage or film. There is a self confidence which comes from being popular. Music is soothing to this individual even as a baby. Behind the peaceful appearance is determination which does not like to be thwarted or opposed.

Venus Novile Pluto — This native is so painstaking in his cr her investigations that he often loses out to some more aggressive examiner. There is great deductive reasoning power and a quality of involvement which leads to eventual success. Endurance and commitment are revealed at an early age.

Noviles of Mars:

Mars Novile Ceres — Individuals with this natal aspect prefer obscurity to fame. They enjoy watching the workings of Mother Nature and recording any variations from normal procedure of both man and the universe. Often he or she has a whimsical sense of humor.

Mars Novile Pallas Athena — A natural sense of rhythm is present in this native. This talent can be developed into a successful career when promoted by parents and child alike. Any creative movement using the repetition of an accent appeals to him or her. This includes jazz, martial marches, rhyming poetry, dancing or sailing among others.

Mars Novile Juno — There is a dignity of movement which attracts confidence in this person. Rather withdrawn in personal relationships, the native is cordial and correct in business dealings. He or she often deals with financial problems, consulting with individuals or firms about the best ways to invest their monies. The native prefers to use one of the medias to inform clients rather than face-to-face confrontations.

Mars Novile Vesta — Standing up for one's own beliefs against popular opinion can lead to being lonely as this native learns early in life. He or she likes best to be in control of the situation but has the fortitude to stand alone when necessary. There is a strong determination to work toward an expressed goal no matter how long it takes. The temperament is a bit aggressive and does not shy away from competition.

Mars Novile Jupiter — These contemplative natives are often remembered after their deaths for unselfish actions on behalf of other people. A inner self-knowledge seems to free them from concern with personal problems in order to better see the plight of those who are less fortunate. He or she perceives the true nature of an activity even as a child. In this way errors are kept to a minimum.

Mars Novile Saturn — With firm action more than one native with this aspect brought freedom to a large group of people, not for personal gain but out of honest compassion. A stroke of the pen may be used to sign legal documents or it may just as effectively write about the dilemma of the oppressed. Whether in public or private life this individual has the security to stand firm in his or her convictions.

Mars Novile Uranus — Sudden injury or illness can be turned into creative endeavors when there is enough resolution of purpose. For many individuals with this natal aspect forced changes in their physical activities made it possible for them to have more time for study and writing. Being born with this planetary combination gives an innovative mind which will rechannel energy into other courses when the normal flow is blocked. This aspect is basically one of optimism.

Mars Novile Neptune — Idealistic principles must be tested at times or so it seems in the life of this native. In cases this fosters a form of religious crusader while in others these tendencies manifest more as a quiet, coaxing manner. There is always present the patience to nurture whatever is necessary to dissolve the problems at hand.

Mars Novile Pluto — Energy is usually released through physical work for the person having this combination of planets in the natal horoscope. In many cases, he or she will follow in the professional field of one of the parents.

Noviles of Jupiter:

Jupiter Novile Ceres — This individual is fundamentally a religious person who will not compromise principles without great pressure or important cause. He or she has the endurance to await the return of order before beginning to build anew. By comprehending the cycles of nature this native has reason to caution others about the aftereffects of both gluttony and miserliness. They influence best through serving others.

Jupiter Novile Pallas Athena — This practical philosopher is often multi-professional being occupied with various projects simultaneously. Writing talents can be refined and honed into prize-winning journalism with this natal aspect. This is one of the aspects denoting fame and success unless denied elsewhere in the horoscope.

Jupiter Novile Juno — Harboring hopes of power and grandeur is not enough to make them come true unless combined with hard work and determination. If this desire for splendor is allowed to get the upper hand before the groundwork for success has been well laid it can lead to disappointment and tragedy. It is well for this native to observe the setting hen who follows through all the established procedure and time before seeing the results of her labor.

Jupiter Novile Vesta — This is the aspect of the good and faithful servant who tends his or her duties diligently over the years looking for neither praise nor reward. However, that does not mean that this aspect will not be found in horoscopes of famous persons who sincerely handle their positions of power with loyalty and steadfastness.

Jupiter Novile Saturn — Physical appearance is striking in most cases when this combination of energies is found in the natal horoscope. There is a grace and grandeur of movement due to excellent bone structure or good alignment of the skeletal frame. When developed by proper training of the rest of the body this native can excel in physical occupations such as gymnastics, dancing, skating or athletics to mention a few. Poise is an obvious attribute regardless of training.

Jupiter Novile Uranus — Even though this native desires to be completely just he or she is curious about who really deserves to win. There may be some unique methods of settling legal matters during this native's lifetime, as well as unexpected revelations because of such occurrences. Regardless of background he or she will have an attitude of authority which will gain respect from peers and superiors alike.

Jupiter Novile Neptune — This native incubates fundamental religious precepts against the time when they can be used or are needed to become public. He or she gathers such curiosities as icons, religious hangings, old manuscripts, and sacred beads into a safe place during times of disaster or persecution of that particular sect. Sooner or later the person will make a final break with organized groups to form a nucleus of a new unit. As a child this native intuitively knows the difference between basic truths and distortions.

Jupiter Novile Pluto — Being sympathetic to the masses makes this native become quite philosophical in his or her approach to life. They often appear to change the present social and economic balance around them in subtle ways. It is almost as though this person wants to be involved in hatching a revolution whether on a world-wide scale or just in the immediate family.

Noviles of Saturn, Uranus, Neptune and Pluto:

Because the slower moving planets create major and minor aspects only during certain years or periods the Noviles for Saturn, Uranus, Neptune and Pluto will be considered in their respective time frames. Persons born during various years react against the background of historical events as well as to the energies in the natal horoscope.

Saturn Novile Uranus — The Twentieth Century began with a separating 40-degree aspect between these two outer bodies in our solar system, followed by a repeat of this aspect in 1946 and again in 1994. As expected there were growth and adjustment periods during the two past aspects as we would anticipate in the one yet to come. Many people born during both of the earlier times inherited positions of authority from family businesses and were required to bring earlier dreams to fulfillment. At both the turn of the century and after World War II countries all over the globe were beginning to develop new alignments, new economic patterns and new social structures. Even the family was undergoing change as a basic unit of society.

Saturn was approaching Uranus at the Novile aspect during 1937 and 1938 when the germs of war were hatching both in Europe and the Far East. These two planets will once again be in the approaching 40-degree aspect in 1994; a time when many soothsayers have predicted change and tragedy.

Saturn Novile Neptune — Numerous intuitive and sensitive people were born while Saturn was approaching Novile to Neptune in 1913 and again in 1949. As these people have grown to maturity there have been waves of interest in occult and metaphysical phenomena in this country and overseas. With the first group there was primarily an interest in spiritualism and materialism; while with development of the second wave there is more interest in evolution of personal psychic traits. The next such aspect occurs in 1985.

During the separating Novile between Saturn and Neptune which occurred in 1921 and again in 1957 new methods of farming which had been developed over the decades came into common usage. It was time for the rebirth of a system of agriculture which would support changing world population, each time forced by near famine in separate parts of the globe. This aspect returns during the middle of the last decade of this century.

Saturn Novile Pluto — One of the factors which the years 1911, 1943 and 1978 had in common was changes in the world currency rates. All of these three approaching Noviles were periods of facing the aftereffects of years of overuse of resources. Yet they were years when faith was rekindled and people lived in hope of better days to come.

Saturn was separating from Pluto at 40 degrees during 1918 and 1950 both when wars were being initiated, once in Europe and once in Asia. In both cases there was the growth of new concepts of leadership attempting to overthrow the existing structure. This aspect reappears during the year 1987.

Uranus Novile Neptune — The only 40-degree aspect occurring between these two outer planets was in the mid 1970's when Uranus approached Neptune. As an applying position there was a birth of new religious and philosophic concepts coming out of a century of writings and investigations. Orthodox churches made permanent changes in their rituals and clerical requirements as a result of part of this manifestation. Ecumenical movements reached their peak of activity. Esoterically speaking many persons called this period "the opening of the veils" when metaphysical teachings begame easier to obtain than in previous time periods.

Uranus Novile Pluto — These two planets were in approaching aspect during the early part of the 1950's during the Korean War and will be separating at this angle during 1983. If nothing else constructive can be said about war it is certainly a time when cultural barriers are broken down rapidly. During the time when American and European servicemen were stationed in this Asian country they became aware of traditions and beliefs of this ancient race as well as of some of the more primitive living conditions existing in other parts of the world.

Neptune Novile Pluto — The single Novile aspect between Neptune and Pluto during this century occurred during the middle of the 1920's when the world was feeling successful and secure after the end of World War I. Powerful companies were being developed from recent inventions, travel and communication was increasing because of the greater use of new fuels, women's lib was beginning its long range change of the female image, and the social class system was undergoing drastic revision in all the European countries. This separating aspect does incubate changes and dissolve the existing structures world wide.

11

Semi-Square Aspect

In addition to causing minor stress or crises, the Semi-Square, or 45-degree aspect, may be considered an additional stimulator in the horoscope. By relating the major activators of the chart - squares, oppositions and conjunctions - to triggers of primary muscle responses the Semi-Square can be compared to the effect on the body of additional stimulants like chemicals or caffeine, friction of increased nerve impulses, discordant music or inharmonious color tones, and irritation from prolonged emotional stress.

69

Even though most action aspects bring varying degrees of unpleasantness they are necessary for the creative process just as both mother and baby must undergo a certain amount of stress and discomfort during the hours of labor before birth. However, the final results are usually worth any frustration or pain involved.

The Semi-Square may be further compared to the activities and tension involved when two armies are maneuvering into position for actual combat. It is the first moment of actually perceiving the possible dangers and differences for both groups.

As a Semi-Square aspect is formed by dividing a 360-degree circle into eight equal segments it can also be called the Eighth Harmonic or a further division of the Fourth Harmonic of Action. Persons who are familiar with the 90-degree dial of Cosmobiology or Uranian Astrology use this concept. An orb of 2 or 3 degrees is usually given when planets are considered in the Semi-Square aspect. This same aspect is also termed the Oktil or Octile, especially in German astrology texts.

Glyph: ∠

Keywords of the Semi-Square:

abrasive	conflict	enthusiasm	irritation
activity	contrast	friction	lacks
adjustments	courage	frown	martial
ambitious	determination	frustration	needs
annoying	detour	grating	pursuits
antagonism	difficulties	hard	resolves
attunement	discord	hastens	stimulator
bumpy road	dynamic	impulsive	stress
challenge	earnings	inflames	tension
clearing	effort	initial effort	unaware
clumsy	engagement (as gears)	irksome	upsets

Semi-Squares of the Sun:

Sun Semi-Square Moon — This person may be born into unfortunate family circumstances which cause him or her to work harder for luxuries other people take for granted. There is pain through associates, usually minor emotional upsets. Family demands that the responsibilities for relatives be taken on at a comparatively early age. Nevertheless there is a strong determination to succeed despite difficulties.

Sun Semi-Square Mercury — This aspect is not possible in the natal horoscope because of the orbital patterns of Mercury around the Sun.

Sun Semi-Square Venus — Lack of appreciation of gifts and affection leads to being ignored by loved ones. This person is usually less gracious than should be expected from family standards and upbringing. Musical talents will have few outlets. When he or she feels unappreciated he is curt with close friends and relatives. Females with this aspect are sometimes lacking in feminine attributes or characteristics. Insecurity can lead to overspending, especially on expensive clothing.

Sun Semi-Square Mars — Clumsiness causes foolish-seeming falls and accidents without serious results. The native should quit blaming others for his own lack of energy and enthusiasm. Sudden spurts of activity such as jogging or running leave the native short of breath because he is not in shape. Infections often need minor surgery to clear up. This person is frequently an innocent victim because he or she chanced to be near the chaos. They tend to be venturesome.

Sun Semi-Square Ceres — Some persons find it more difficult to break habits made in childhood than others. Out of this hesitancy to leave behind the security of early days comes minor problems with intestinal upsets. When in situations of stress this native reacts from instinct. He or she may be overly concerned with bodily modesty.

Sun Semi-Square Pallas Athena — People who constantly find fault with their current job status are born with this minor aspect. They may also be either drawn to the wearing of uniforms or completely repulsed by the idea. Often they find need for further training into the technical aspects of their career just when they expect a promotion. There is a constant sense of searching.

Sun Semi-Square Juno — Women with this aspect often wear either an excess of jewelry and cosmetics or none at all, with almost a phobia about same. This aspect brings a restriction of freedom of body movements which does not inhibit activity but looks awkward. Mate or friends often shock this person by minor social offenses. There are overreactions to most situations.

Sun Semi-Square Vesta — The seeking of a spot of peace and quiet in the midst of celebrations is common. This native seems to be out of phase with the social activities around him or her. Learning to share in the little joys of life would be helpful. Usually there is a quiet, unassuming appearance.

Sun Semi-Square Jupiter — Empathy for those who are suffering is brought about by personal periods of illness. There is a religious passion bordering on a missionary urge to hasten reforms. By inheriting a fortunate place in life there are also the demanding duties and responsibilities which go with such a role. Successful people often rue the lack of time for privacy and family enjoyment.

Sun Semi-Square Saturn — Persons with this aspect are censored for things which they have not done. Support can be withheld for failures over which the native has no control. There are detours or temporary setbacks in professional endeavors. Eventually he or she finds an unusual way to achieve when normal avenues are closed.

Sun Semi-Square Uranus — Courageous but impractical, these people learn by trial and error. Freedom of action is often thwarted by reactions to their own exaggerated enthusiasm. Impulsiveness is more natural than caution or propriety.

Sun Semi-Square Neptune — A sense of fear which sometimes expresses by telling "little white lies" results in frequent scoldings even as an adult. By trusting the wrong person this native often gets hurt. He or she feels victimized by any doubts shown by close friends or mate. Musical ability comes to fruition only after much difficulty and delay.

Sun Semi-Square Pluto — People in general seem plodding and slow to accept new ideas from this person. Because of this he chooses to prod the public with any means possible, sometimes resulting in adverse reactions. With this love of using shock techniques he or she then wonders why plans backfire.

Semi-Squares of the Moon:

Moon Semi-Square Mercury — Blunt speech can come across as crude from this person who lacked parental affection as a child. This native learns to think and speak quickly because of pressing needs. Blackouts from malnutrition cause damage to nerve endings in extreme cases. They are possibly deserted or mistreated as children. These people are not the most careful of automobile drivers.

Moon Semi-Square Venus — Easily wounded by careless words and actions of others the native learns to be protective of his or her own interests. He misses actual opportunities to be loved because of constant dreaming about the ideal romance. Complaints about lack of luxury items is a symptom of inner discontent.

Moon Semi-Square Mars — Acting before thinking out all the small details clearly results in getting caught up in disturbing situations time after time. This person frequently gets small burns from chemicals or matches. An irritated mother creates the early habit of fussing at others as release for his or her own emotional tension. Destructive habits are difficult to change once they are ingrained.

Moon Semi-Square Ceres — Trust and faith are tested many times during the lifetime. As a child this native may be adopted or feel alienated from his or her biological parents. There is an unusual amount of dependence on one or another of the grandparents. At times he or she will be fanatic about food fads.

Moon Semi-Square Pallas Athena — This native often grows up to be a working mother or is the child of a career woman. He or she learns early to channel emotions into physical tasks rather than complain, almost to the point of being a workaholic. When involved in one of the numerous causes for equality which he or she will espouse throughout the years this person becomes adamant about the importance of an issue. During these periods it is useless to try to detract them by suggesting other interests.

Moon Semi-Square Juno — Frustration caused when other people don't follow the same dedication to pomp and ceremony can ruin many a party for this native. A great deal of nervous tension caused by overconcern with little details manifests in headaches or digestive upsets. Let this person enjoy crying at weddings and funerals to his or her heart's content. An easier aspect for a woman to handle in today's society, where men are expected to hide emotions.

Moon Semi-Square Vesta — Many years may be spent in seeking to provide a substitute for the parental affection missing during early childhood. This native defends his or her personal beliefs even to the point of alienating close family and friends. In some cases there are allergies to milk or dairy products.

Moon Semi-Square Jupiter — Honesty with self is the big lesson to learn for someone having this natal aspect. There is the tendency to stretch time too thin to do anything really well. He or she takes on excessive obligations because of a certain misunderstanding of public demands.

Moon Semi-Square Saturn — There exists a lack of complete assurance in this person's own innate abilities. Because of this he or she is constantly trying to analyze and explain every action. This can lead to being overly apologetic about imagined faults. When criticized or corrected by a superior or an older person the native will often react with excessive anger followed by depression. Mainly an aspect of self doubt.

Moon Semi-Square Uranus — Sometimes people are involved in fighting for freedoms and rights which they would not know how to handle if they were received. So it is with this native who never really seems to know what he or she wants. It is best to avoid controversy whenever possible. Emotional reactions to changes are usually squelched by those in positions of authority.

Moon Semi-Square Neptune — Often a lack of clarity manifests as the "absent-minded professor" syndrome, thus letting someone else handle the minute details of daily life. This person is usually unclear about commitments, either emotional or financial.

Moon Semi-Square Pluto — Absolute frankness is appropriate on very few occasions as these natives are prone to learn time after time. There is also lack of fear of public censure in this aspect so that it shows up as nursing wounded soldiers on the battlefield, entertaining transvestites in social gatherings, writing gruesome details of murder in local newspaper and wearing shocking attire to prove a point, to name a few examples.

Semi-Squares of Mercury:

Mercury Semi-Square Venus — Aggressive women who are quite involved in their career advancement may take out insecure feelings by yelling at their children. Upon occasions this aspect indicates replacing one's mate at his or her chosen profession. A sharp tongue hides hurt feelings and lack of confidence. There is a certain mental ambivalence. Wishful thinking causes irritability when it is not understood and fulfilled by others. This native will sacrifice creature comforts for future glory.

Mercury Semi-Square Mars — Because a dictatorial attitude irritates people this authoritative manner works against the person. Used more positively it can be a real asset in getting ahead. Because of the unconscious trend to create dissention in groups there is need to learn to cope gracefully with uncomfortable situations.

Mercury Semi-Square Ceres — Enriching the speech with local cliches can be both confusing and appealing to others. Getting to the point quickly makes communication seem almost brusque. When this native is around people from other areas or foreign countries he or she will rapidly adopt their accent or manner of speaking. This is an unconscious habit, not meant to mimic another.

Mercury Semi-Square Pallas Athena — Rather than rationalizing one's own shortcomings it would be better for this native to come to grips with them and try to correct some major faults. It will be necessary for him or her to take some form of public speaking or voice training to advance the career. No matter how much he or she enjoys public acclaim he must make it possible for others to be in the spotlight at least part of the time. In other words, do not monopolize conversations so much. This aspect is good for a career as a newswriter or speechwriter for a public figure.

Mercury Semi-Square Juno — There is a tendency to clipped speech due to lack of self confidence. Sometimes this quality is worse because of slight hearing loss. Constant patting of hair or picking of nails shows absence of ease in social situations. Less concern with self and more care of less fortunate people helps control this type of reaction.

Mercury Semi-Square Vesta — Often this person is an only child or there is a great difference between the age of siblings. By concentrating so strongly on one avenue of study to the exclusion of all other fields the native tends to be unaware of many of the issues of the times. There is the tendency to carry on monologues rather than true dialogues with others.

Mercury Semi-Square Jupiter — Complex legal problems crop up from time to time with which the native must deal. These are usually caused by the fact that he or she tends to plunge into situations before gettng all the details. There are often periodic buying sprees or overindulgence in some area of life.

Mercury Semi-Square Saturn — Overcommitment to tasks causes despondency. The native feels tied down by schedules of any type. He or she is often bored by necessary studies or social conversation. There will probably be the need for talking with many older persons during childhood.

Mercury Semi-Square Uranus — A lack of sophistication both gets the native into trouble and out of tight spots. This unaffected manner shows up in speech and writings, as well as in relationships with others. If left alone, the native will follow the "Pied Piper" into dreamland before checking any details or alternative action. He or she gets excited about new ideas and accepts unusual concepts without reservation.

Mercury Semi-Square Neptune — Double meanings elude this native until it is too late to take constructive action. He or she enjoys the mental activity associated with crossword puzzles and word games but is often at a loss to understand clearly defined instructions. When in doubt he may be tempted to use unethical tactics to gain ground in a situation. This type of behavior leads to scandals and even to legal action.

Mercury Semi-Square Pluto — Here is a person who deeply resents anyone else interceding for him or her. Naturally people do this all the time, much to the native's dismay. He or she writes letters of protest to magazines and newspapers frequently. There is a tendency to digress from the main path of thought into side issues which are of little concern to the general public.

Semi-Squares of Venus:

Venus Semi-Square Mars — A need for funds because of impulsive spending sometimes tempts the native to accept money under false pretenses such as politicans receive bribes or sports figures accept money to fix game scores. When these actions come to light they are not favored by others. Intruding on people's privacy makes them angry. There is much discord and impulse in this aspect.

Venus Semi-Square Ceres — Weight fluctuation can be caused by an imbalance in the appetite. When foods are eaten too rapidly the native feels hungry long after he or she has dined because foods are still being assimilated by the body. Use of fresh fruit or unsweetened juices before meals will help eliminate this problem. Self indulgence needs to be curbed or brought under control. A gentle touch shows affection more than erratic assertions of friendship.

Venus Semi-Square Pallas Athena — There is some difficulty in blending various hues and shades together. Just because certain colors are in vogue does not mean that they are appropriate for the native to wear or use. Difficulties with co-workers arise out of jealousy. Whether the problem deals with women's liberation or vacation bonuses it would be wise for this native to learn to share another's happiness rather than to always want the same awards for him or herself.

Venus Semi-Square Juno — Periods of restriction come for everyone so the native must learn to accept them and get on with daily living. There may be long separations from his or her mate because of family responsibilities or job demands. Monies from inheritance can be delayed for legal reasons. There is an interest in the use of hand reflexology.

Venus Semi-Square Vesta — Any inequality is a good reason for this native to crusade for the downtrodden. He or she is a firm believer in helping to release the oppressed from their bondage, whether they want assistance or not. There is need for the clarity of thought which comes through composure. Clarity opens understanding that grows into confidence. It is important to learn the difference between good deeds and meddling.

Venus Semi-Square Jupiter — This aspect brings some good factors such as worrying about the earth's resources as well as some aggravating characteristics such as being boring. There can be a tendency to be overly pretentious about minor achievements. One actor with this aspect even starred in a comedy entitled "Green Acres."

Venus Semi-Square Saturn — Older women are critical of the native's behavior. This person may figuratively or literally kill the thing he loves. There will be temporary delays to success during the years. Any form of teasing causes embarassment and blushing.

Venus Semi-Square Uranus — Being harsh-spoken makes this native unpopular with his or her peers. He or she will promote their own innovative ideas at the price of personal pleasure or security. There is an uncanny ability to be around when discoveries are made or when escapades are occurring.

Venus Semi-Square Neptune — Being easily mislead by false promises of good fortune and happiness leads this native to associate with unsavory characters. There is definite need to learn to be cautious in approaching strangers. However, it is important not to be threatened by one's own fears. When in an emergency he or she is called to help it is not necessary to evade the summons, merely to understand when one really has the power necessary to attract helpers and work together toward success.

Venus Semi-Square Pluto — This native is often forced by circumstances to be the symbol of an age or an idea, from the minor situation of representing a particular holiday on a parade float to being the nation's number one pin-up girl during wartime. Though there is great public appeal there is usually a stormy personal romance. This same charisma which attracts mass attention leads to unpleasant disruptions in the love life.

Semi-Squares of Mars:

Mars Semi-Square Ceres — A hard working individual with a great deal of physical stamina does not mind heavy, outdoor exercise. It is better for this native to follow the old adage of "plenty of rest and good food" rather than depend on vitamins and pep pills. There is the possibility of working as a paramedic or other hospital related professions.

Mars Semi-Square Pallas Athena — When too many jobs are accepted the result is overwork. Zealous desire to achieve leads this native to drive himself or herself beyond the efficient level of producing. Haste makes waste so he or she needs to learn to slow down to be more effective.

Mars Semi-Square Juno — Little is to be obtained by structuring life so tightly that one's partner or mate constantly rebels. This continual warring leaves both parties completely exhausted. Stubborn insistence and expenditure of effort to futile ends only brings resentment and enemies. There is need for much relaxation.

Mars Semi-Square Vesta — Knowing how to eliminate the unnecessary in each current task makes the work load easier. However, this attitude does not win friends and influence people. This urge to accomplish leads to stringent rules for the native. Unusual encounters with men may occur.

Mars Semi-Square Jupiter — Undeserved misfortune is difficult to handle without becoming bitter. There are probably loss of business contacts and contracts brought about by being too aggressive in selling self or a product. Impulsive actions results in carelessness. When the facts are not clearly defined the native seems to be extravagant. Each task must be done for its own sake before going on to another.

Mars Semi-Square Saturn — Fewer mistakes are made when the reason is unselfish. This native must mature by mastering the minor irritations met throughout life. In learning patience he also learns to be master of himself.

Mars Semi-Square Uranus — In one outstanding example of this aspect the native is a well-known reporter who exposes people in positions of authority. He or she loves to be involved in the middle of controversies. No issue is to small to be tackled if it hints at a scandal. This is not a good aspect for a community fund raiser or counselor. Individuals having these two planets related in their chart are looking for excitement.

Mars Semi-Square Neptune — Things are hard to untangle, from knitting yarn to business taxes, for this native. He or she often works with confusing issues. There is the chance of physical abuse at some time during the life span.

Mars Semi-Square Pluto — Feeling abandoned by society there is the danger of this person becoming involved with an underground movement. He or she loves to probe in depth into any concern. When in doubt the verdict will probably go against the native, so he or she should keep a clean slate.

Semi-Squares of Jupiter:

Jupiter Semi-Square Ceres — Advising people with "homespun philosophy" can backfire. It is well to be generous and helpful so long as people are allowed to run their own lives. Charity is only beneficial when it encourages the other person to help him or herself. This native needs to learn to be more severe with self and less critical with others.

Jupiter Semi-Square Pallas Athena — People in positions of power must be careful not to abuse that trust. Desire for being elected to high office is not sufficient recommendation. There must also be a sense of responsibility to one's constituents. This native is advised not to undertake more than he or she is willing to carry out.

Jupiter Semi-Square Juno — The wife who overfeeds her husband fits into the category of this aspect. It is possible to damage or cripple another by doing too much for them. Even when funds are restricted it is better to work hand in hand rather than being overly generous. This aspect suggests that there will be times of both feast and famine for the native in his or her married life.

Jupiter Semi-Square Vesta — Compromise is the secret of gaining others to one's side. Because of the tendency to be overly zealous about an issue this native turns people against both himself and his enterprise. This is a common placement for an evangelist.

Jupiter Semi-Square Saturn — No matter how much he or she makes as a salary there is never enough money for all the desires. This should never be an excuse to tamper with funds belonging to others. Being over-awed by fame makes one very vulnerable to criticism.

Jupiter Semi-Square Uranus — People who argue at the drop of a hat are usually considered scrappy. This fighting spirit is helpful for sports figures and men in battle but a little hard to handle in everyday life. For this native there will be continual trouble and suspensions from his job because of his quick temper. Opportunities open up once the native learns to control his quick tongue.

Jupiter Semi-Square Neptune — Many people with this aspect are drawn to the medical profession. There can be periods of confusion and doubt in the career because they are overly trusting. At times the native may be embarrassed by being considered different from the norm. It is easier not to expect the public to understand one's motives.

Jupiter Semi-Square Pluto — Ideas often materialize in a slightly different form than this native has imagined. He or she will work through setbacks and upsets until the job is finished, no matter how impractical the scheme. Many inventors with this aspect never know the full value of their creative experiments during their life times.

Semi-Squares of Saturn, Uranus, Neptune and Pluto:

Because the slower moving planets create major and minor aspects only during certain years or periods the Semi-Squares for Saturn, Uranus, Neptune and Pluto will be considered in their respective time frames. Persons born during various years react against the background of historical events.

Saturn Semi-Square Uranus — The separating aspect formed during 1903 and 1904 represents many of the changes being brought about by multiple inventions around the turn of the century. Persons born during this time period saw the automobile replace the horse and buggy, electric lights become the common means of illumination instead of gas and oil, airplane travel as the current mode of travel, machines grow from tools of mankind to replacements for most forms of labor, to mention a few of the changes. To undergo such an overhaul during a single lifetime certainly presented stresses and upsets in their security base.

The approaching aspect formed by Saturn and Uranus during 1936 and

1937 saw a complete change in the political climate of the world. This pre-World War II period was full of tension and fear for most of the globe. Persons born in Europe during that period were uprooted from their homes and scattered about. No country remained untouched by the effects of that great upheaval so all persons born during the thirties lived through it to face building a new economic and political structure.

During 1947 when Saturn was separating Semi-Square again from Uranus the world was realigning itself and rebuilding along new lines. Former enemies became token allies. Threat of nuclear warfare overshadowed the celebration of peace and prosperity. Clouds were gathering for long term skirmishes in the Middle East and Asia.

This book is being written before the next approaching Semi-Square between Saturn and Uranus which will occur in 1981, so the historical implications cannot be given. It is, however, even now in time of world wide tension and economic recession caused by many factors such as overpopulation, shortage of natural fuel and oil, loss of crops due to unusual weather conditions, lack of understanding between nations and loss of faith in the future.

The final Semi-Square during this century between these two planets will be formed in 1994 when Saturn separates from Uranus once again. During the approaching Semi-Squares there seems to be a build up of tension while around the separating aspect readjustments are suggested. So it may be for this period at the end of the century.

Saturn Semi-Square Neptune — Approaching Semi-Squares between Saturn and Neptune occurred in the years 1913, 1948 and 1984 during the Twentieth Century. These seemed to be dealing with learning how to adjust to some of the new inventions including man's need to reaffirm his religious faith. For the years of 1921, 1958, 1994 and 1995 Saturn was separating from this aspect with Neptune. The first two periods dealt with economic reverses and also with drug abuse. In America the twenties were years of alcohol prohibition and the late fifties were concerned with stopping the flow of illegal drugs into the country. Perhaps there will be an immediate concern with changing some of the overuse of medical or prescription drugs during the last aspect.

Saturn Semi-Square Pluto — The war years are well defined by the 45-degree aspect which centered around 1911, 1918 and 1919, 1943, 1951, 1977 and 1988. Because of the slow movement plus retrogradation minor aspects with Pluto overlap through several years duration. World-wide upheaval placed its stamp on all natives born in these past eventful years when homes, families and society in general were completely changed. The results of the 1988 aspect remain to be seen.

Uranus Semi-Square Neptune — The single time when Uranus and Neptune were 45 degrees apart during the 1900's was during 1973 and 1974 with Uranus approaching a conjunction with Neptune to occur later in the century. There was a certain amount of detachment concerned with religious endeavors. Some esotericists inferred that this aspect related to a lifting of the hidden veils of the spiritual hierarchy. It certainly was a period when many people expressed an interest in occult phenomenon. Numerous metaphysical centers and bookstores opened in public shopping areas, classes were taught in neighborhood schools and churches, the mass media opened its doors to astrologers and spiritualists, and cycles were discussed candidly in newspapers and on television interview shows. Optional belief systems brought stress and discomfort to a rather conservative nation as Buddhism, Zen, Shinto and other oriental philosophies introduced ideas into the Western culture. Traditional Christian churches were caught temporarily off balance and needed to readjust their priorities.

Uranus Semi-Square Pluto — As these two heavy planets were in a stress aspect during the years of 1948 and 1949 when the world was recuperating from a great World War periods of tension and difficulties would be expected. Alliances were realigning, economies needed boosting, people felt out of step with reality, irksome conditions prevailed, nations were beginning to perceive their differences with one another, political groups were maneuvering into position for the coming conflicts, and there was a general atmosphere of discord. The next semi-square aspect between Uranus and Pluto will occur in 1986 and 1987 when Uranus will be moving away from the slower Pluto position. This departing aspect usually deals with difficulty with natural resources so it would seem the world is due for some upheaval in that area. Lack of forethought has led nations to misplace their priorities so that there is the possibility of severe depletion of oil, coal, timber and food. Indeed this aspect would suggest a bumpy road ahead. Out of this challenge, however, could come many innovative ideas and much creative action so that there are two sides of this picture.

Neptune Semi-Square Pluto — During the years 1928 through 1931 many countries of the world were immersed in economic depression. This stressful aspect did indeed clear the ground for political changes to come. Some were more effective than others in resolving the primary difficulties. The earning ability of masses of people was permanently affected. Some individuals faced the dilemma with strong resolve to work around the situation while others felt victimized by their circumstances. However, the events of these years made their mark on all who lived through them.

12

Septile Aspect

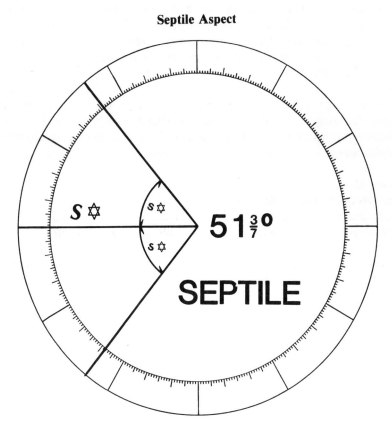

One of the most difficult aspects to see unless found by exact calculation of the longitudinal distance between planets the Septile measures 51-3/7 degrees. This particular angle is formed by dividing a 360-degree circle by the number seven. Most research with the Septile has been done under the asupices of the field called Harmonics. The earliest and best known research with the Seventh Harmonic was that of John Addey's investigation of some four thousand plus British clergy.

Any affiliation with the number seven is immediately suspected of having religious connotations because of that long-time definition through the study of Numerology. There is also the possibility of wanting to work alone, to be unobserved or not to be readily available to the general public.

In this research the Septile has shown trends toward being the time of realignment following a minor setback or upset when planets are in separating aspect. The approaching 51-3/7-degree aspect shows more the tendency toward demanding a personal commitment after a major testing period. This often requires one or more sacrifices on the part of the native. By example, this period could be compared with the tradition of a captain lashing himself to the mast of his ship in time of extreme distress. A reliable leader would undertake such a move only after he had done all in his earthly power to procure the safety of both ship and crew. At which time the wise and faithful captain must place his trust entirely in a Higher Power and give himself up to the inevitable. Whether he survives or perishes lies in God's hands.

There is not sufficient research to present delineations for all the planets in Septile aspect to all others so the following keywords will be all that is contained in this particular book. An orb of 1 or 2 degrees is usually given for this aspect.

Glyph: ✿

Keywords of the Septile:

commitment	focusing	narrow	random
continuing	inevitable	occult	religious
depth	inner	original	symbolic
disrupts	karmic	perverts	unpredictable
fixation	liberates	quiet	unseen

13

Sextile Aspect

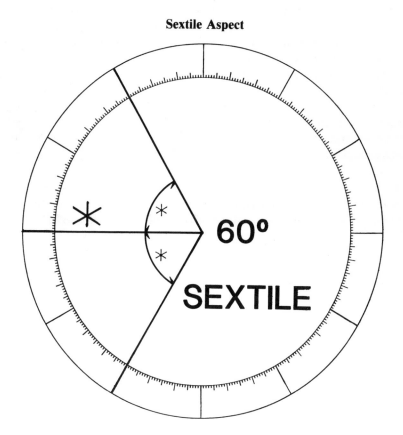

60°

SEXTILE

Like a friendly puppy the Sextile is there to help only if he is trained correctly. It can be very useful after some effort is exerted to train the potential
or use the opportunities which are presented. Often the Sextile brings supportive people into a sphere of influence.

This aspect is formed by the division of the 360-degree circle into six
equal portions or can be termed to be part of the Sixth Harmonic of influence. The Sextile is created from an angular distance of 60 degrees between planets and is one-half the distance of the trine thus being related to

the same rather inactive family of aspects.

A separating 60-degree angle shows spontaneous appearance of ideas or inventive concepts such as happens from dreams or moments of inspiration. The same aspect when planets are approaching toward conjunction with each other shows more a perception of universal principles.

The Sextile aspect may be likened to the soft, warm breeze of spring which drifts across the face bringing pleasant scents of apple blossoms in its wake. That same soft stirring also carries the pollen from flower to flower with its potential of fertilizing the budding plant.

Mr. Charles Jayne, renown American astrologer, has likened the horoscope which contains a number of Sextile aspects scattered through it to the formation of a supportive Cradle pattern which makes the native dependent on family and friends for support.

Because of the wealth of material on the Sextile aspect to be found in other astrology texts only the following keywords will be considered here. The orb to be used should be the one given by the author of the specific book being read.

Glyph: ✶
Keywords of the Sextile:

application	friendly	intuitive	potential
cooperative	harmonious	lucky	practical
dreams	ideas	opportunity	relaxed
dull	intellectual	perceptive	soft

14

Quintile Aspect

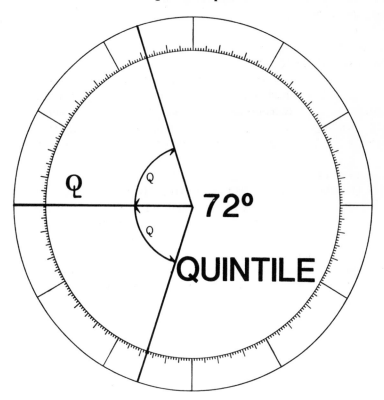

When a 360-degree circle is divided into five equal parts the 72-degree, or Quintile, aspect is formed. Thus this angle is part of the abundant research which has recently been done on the Fifth Harmonic.

Numerous articles and books contain opinions about the esoteric or karmic delineations of planets in Quintile aspect with each other. There is even speculation about use of this 72-degree aspect in mystery schools of the past. Perhaps the term esoteric should be taken literally as "hidden, not obvious." Then it would be easily understood that when separations between planets are not multiples of 30 they are not immediately visible when scanning degrees in the horoscope.

Without exception astrologers who have investigated the Quintile aspect found that it related to inborn talents or skills concerning the planets involved. To a further degree this aspect shows how information derived through the senses is registered and utilized by the human mind. Because the Quintile denotes use and manifestation of inborn traits it may fundamentally be defined as being in tune with the vibrations of the moment. This is like hearing the silent resonance of God's world in harmony and being able to express this sensation to others.

An orb of 1 to 3 degrees is usually given for this particular aspect in the natal horoscope.

Glyph: Q
Keywords of the Quintile:

ability	cultured	management	self-assertion
art	discipleship	manifestation	specialize
channels	exceptional	mastery	talent
comprehending	insight	originality	understanding
creativity	interrelatedness	penetration	uniqueness

Quintiles of the Sun:

Sun Quintile Moon — When an individual is born with this aspect he or she expresses inner emotions vividly and dramatically. There is tremendous inner drive. As well as being idealistic about human potential in general the person instinctively blends the masculine aggressiveness and the feminine receptivity into a unique style of expression.

Sun Quintile Mercury — This aspect is not possible in the natal horoscope because of the orbital patterns of Mercury around the Sun.

Sun Quintile Venus — This aspect is not possible in the natal horoscope because of the orbital patterns of Venus around the Sun.

Sun Quintile Mars — This native transforms energies into refined channels of expression. Transforming an old folk dance into contemporary rage is only one of these possibilities. By learning to discipline raw passion or energy he or she readjusts the very aura around his body, and thus other people's responses.

Sun Quintile Ceres — Being friendly and companionable attracts that same reaction from friends and associates. Using wisdom this native knows to find the right time to suggest universal goals to others. He or she shares a feeling of mutual respect with even those for whom he cares.

Sun Quintile Pallas Athena — From this natal aspect comes a strong sense of determination which needs to achieve material success and renown. In amusing or serving the public this person clarifies universal truths by veiling them in clever sayings. He or she is capable of immersing himself completely in each task which is the path to real mastery of a project. There is contentment in accomplishing a goal whether it be through playing children's games, finishing a day's work, completing a tax form or publishing a book, to mention a few examples.

Sun Quintile Juno —Being conservative in appearance and methodical in approach this native often steps into an inherited position of wealth and rank. An excellent natal placement for one who would be interested in the diplomatic service on any level. This native is instinctively aware of the proper etiquette and protocol for the moment.

Sun Quintile Vesta — There is a sense of knowing when to retreat from an impossible situation witout losing face when these two planets are in Quintile in the natal horoscope. Always ready to serve and take on his or her share of hard work the native realizes when it is wise to cease attacking an insurmountable obstacle.

Sun Quintile Jupiter — Both leadership and religious fervor are present in an individual having this natal combination. Because of the intimate involvement with a search for cosmic or religious principles this native often marries or becomes closely allied with members of the clergy. There may be an ability to be prophetic or simply a well developed intuition. He or she knows how to appeal to people's emotions and how to rouse an audience to be sympathetic. Some people with this aspect write about theological concepts and theories.

Sun Quintile Saturn — Persons having this natal aspect are usually well rewarded by the world for their years of hard work and preparation. There is need for periods of withdrawal to develop a clear judgment and unblemished perception. A quiet, contemplative child who usually grows into a dignified, discerning adult.

Sun Quintile Uranus — Such a new age leader must be intuitive but cautious for people will listen and believe what the native is saying. There are fleeting moments of true insight which are translated into dramatic revelations for the masses. It is important for this individual to squelch any impulse to take drastic measures to achieve his or her own goal. Patience and truth will out in the long run.

Sun Quintile Neptune — A person born with this combination of planets in the natal horoscope enjoys the ritualistic part of a religious service without being told of the symbolism behind each act. In the same manner of expression there is the ability to be a fine method actor or actress simply by emoting the inner feelings aroused by suggestion of certain actions.

Sun Quintile Pluto — Quite often people with this aspect are born into one culture but must be moved because of conditions beyond their own control. They simply accept such upheaval as part of the general upheaval of life. With an inborn charisma this native can easily influence other people about both great and small issues.

Quintiles of the Moon:

Moon Quintile Mercury — When this particular combination of planetary energies is present in the natal horoscope the native knows how to develop and use the emotions to enhance communications with others. Sometimes he or she develops a method of contacting a special friend or relative in their own special code. Words often have double meanings for this individual.

Moon Quintile Venus — Having a sensitive body and mind this person knows how to express undying love and appreciation so the loved one can understand. Often there is a spiritual regeneration of the physical desires with this natal aspect. He or she will set aside personal wishes to help another. There is a deep and abiding faith beneath whatever exterior the native wears.

Moon Quintile Mars — Being a champion of the underdog often sets one in the position of being outspoken about his or her own personal feelings. This native, who is a strong advocate of equality for all, often finds himself or herself in such a situation. This natal aspect represents a strong and intense need for personal freedom.

Moon Quintile Ceres — Having natural stage presence comes in handy at all public gatherings, not just in the theater. This native encourages a more realistic approach to any artistic endeavors. He or she prefers to remain in the background and let someone else have the starring role. This is a gentle aspect unless denied elsewhere in the horoscope.

Moon Quintile Pallas Athena — This very stable person is able to penetrate the emotional shields which people put up to protect themselves. He or she can sublimate personal feelings when necessary to complete a job or seem more professional in attitude. Although sometimes accused of being cold and heartless the native is proud of personal achievements. An objective aspect, especially when found in a female chart.

Moon Quintile Juno — Often a person with this natal combination manages to transform his or her life through an unusual marriage arrangement. He or she knows that any show of vanity will only result in tears and humiliation so he keeps his sense of dignity at all times. This individual can benefit greatly from self-analysis and grow from the knowledge obtained. There is usually immense emotional control through long practice and training.

Moon Quintile Vesta — This is the stuff of which heroes are made. Persons with this combination of planets in the natal horoscope are often noted for their exceptional bravery in the face of disaster. This can be on a large scale or as local as rescuing the neighbor's kitten from a tall tree. There is the ability to put aside personal fears in order to carry out an immediate need.

Moon Quintile Jupiter — With understanding this individual is able to master emotional outbursts. As basic truths unfold throughout life he or she learns about non-personal compassion and healing. Sometimes there is an interest in studying natural methods of bringing the body into alignment and good health.

Moon Quintile Saturn — An individual with this natal aspect can bring dreams into reality. He or she gives off the warmth of a true spirtual server. A reasonable person with a sensible attitude toward the problems of life this native can penetrate to the very core of a situation in order to find the most effective solution. There is the ability to look at great social changes in a simple, childlike fashion.

Moon Quintile Uranus — With determination and courage this native can pull himself or herself back from the depths of depression to conquer even physical disabilities. He or she knows how to make good come out of tragedy. When sudden accidents or illnesses strike he exerts self control to change life goals to fit the new circumstances.

Moon Quintile Neptune — This native can literally infold an audience into accepting figments of his or her imagination as actuality. Being sympathetic to new causes he is often supportive of undercover groups which are involved in interesting research or study. This person understands complicated medical problems whether or not he can explain them in professional terminology. There is the ability to open new worlds to others through personal experience.

Moon Quintile Pluto — Living through personal trauma is one way in which this native learns to develop the soul. It becomes necessary for him or her to learn to respect authority and become resourceful in protecting himself. By remaining outwardly calm they can practice overcoming emotional outbursts in difficult periods.

Quintiles of Mercury:

Mercury Quintile Venus — This childlike trust is difficult for other people to understand and respect. A person with such a natal aspect is quite original in expressing himself or herself but prefers to exhibit a friendly, simple outlook to the world. Blessed with a natural wit he or she often adopts a scatterbrained manner which endears him to audiences and friends alike. This native conquers the tendency to worry through spiritual meditation or prayer.

Mercury Quintile Mars — A hard hitting individual whether involved in business, sports or politics. This native belts right out at the problems or grievances being voiced around him or her. While he or she can be quite sophisticated when the occasion demands he prefers to lounge informally with close friends and associates. This person knows instinctively how to persevere until a lasting agreement is reached.

Mercury Quintile Ceres — There is a strong sense of national pride when this combination of planets is found in the natal horoscope. Sometimes such a native is called upon to protect ancient theories and writings by copying and translating them into the language of the day. If necessary the individual makes a good foot soldier in time of war or national disaster.

Mercury Quintile Pallas Athena — With patience and persistence this native can penetrate the veil behind which people hide. An exuberant speaker he or she is gypsy-like in enjoying spur of the moment of travel. This person likes to enlist others to work on personal pet projects so there is always a cluster of people around. There is no false modesty to prevent this individual from openly displaying the talents of either himself or a capable student. This is a good aspect for a teacher, especially one who works with handicapped children through the medium of art or handicrafts.

Mercury Quintile Juno — A charming way of expressing himself or herself may include the affectation of a foreign accent for this native. Publicly charming, witty and intelligent this native gains respect for his or her wisdom by basing teachings on a solid foundation. He or she quickly comprehends a changing social emphasis and adapts to the current moment. Thus, he is in constant demand by friends and audiences alike.

Mercury Quintile Vesta — This native is more concerned with keeping traditions of the past than in exploring new fields. He or she is a gentle conversationalist with soft and pleasing voice. A childlike appearance and winning smile hide the ambitions of a very determined individual.

Mercury Quintile Jupiter — Often a mathematician or prolific writer this native can interpret cosmic concepts for easier understanding by a larger audience. He or she is able to use pictures and graphs to represent ideas which fill pages of prose explanation. There is an inborn grasp of the meanings behind metaphysical teachings. In some cases these individuals revived old legends or folk tales and set them to music. By thus making such material a part of the daily experience more people will listen and comprehend.

Mercury Quintile Saturn — True humility is not a quality belonging solely to the poor and impoverished. Some wealthy financiers and reformers are blessed with this very trait, shown by such a combination of planetary energies in the natal horoscope. Regardless of the station in life this individual is interested in the problems of those who suffer. He or she is a wise person who will not attempt anything that is beyond his or her strength or authority to achieve. Therefore, reforms begun by this individual will be put into action as soon as it is feasible to do so.

Mercury Quintile Uranus — With this balance of planetary energies in the natal horoscope comes the desire to roam throughout the land and explore little known sites of interest. Such a native is apt to develop an interest in ecology by observing nature in its unspoiled state. He or she may spend hours observing various animals or birds in order to learn more about their habits.

Mercury Quintile Neptune — An excellent aspect for a mystery writer because this person's private thoughts remain unfathomable for associates and close friends alike. This native can mesh reality with illusions as well as any magician.

Mercury Quintile Pluto — Such a wise man fosters fellowship and humane ideals by voicing universal goals. This individual knows how to appeal to the common fears and anxieties of the public. He or she can easily arouse sympathy for an important cause.

Quintiles of Venus:

Venus Quintile Mars — A desire to be a famous world traveler emerges from this native even as a child. He or she may manage to achieve this dream through joining one of the military services as a career or by becoming somewhat of a celebrity in his or her own field of interest. Attempts at communicating are brief and to the point.

Venus Quintile Ceres — Handsome men and beautiful women need little makeup or knowledge of dress to make them appealing. This photogenic native is born with poise and good looks. In addition, having a sense of humor makes him or her pleasant to be around.

Venus Quintile Pallas Athena — Being calm in the face of tumult takes a certain kind of temperament. This native knows how to take the best of two worlds and leave the rest behind. An organized business leader, a political liaison between two factions or the family stalwart all need to be able to smooth troubled waters in times of tension.

Venus Quintile Juno — Having a unique style of expression does not keep this person from being dignified. There may possibly be an unusual manner of walking or standing which draws attention to the native. This difference only enhances the natural charm with which the individual was born.

Venus Quintile Vesta — A person born with this aspect in the horoscope knows fully the meaning of sacrifice of luxury and love for a purpose. He or she may use family background or wealth to explore new ideas and beliefs. In reality this native is only revitalizing old traditions for future benefit to mankind.

Venus Quintile Jupiter — This is definitely one of the aspects denoting possible fame and fortune for the native. There is a strong sense of the dramatic which can be trained into an asset for either an author or a playwright. Usually this individual will hone any talents to a fine point which can be called into use momentarily when needed. On the lighter side, he or she has a green thumb and enjoys working around plants and vegetables. There is an innate understanding of the cycles of life.

Venus Quintile Saturn — Nothing is as pleasurable to this native as working with the elderly to share some of the joys of youth. Music has a calming effect when the individual needs to be soothed. He or she may study under a major guru at some period during the life. Eventually the person will develop his or her own theory of order all the while suggesting social reform of one form or another.

Venus Quintile Uranus — An enjoyable person to be around, this native can develop excitement out of the simple daily events of life. This is also a good aspect for one to have who nurses the wounded in times of disaster. In one way or another this individual will always be helping the less fortunate.

Venus Quintile Neptune — This unselfish individual must indeed be watched over by guardian angels. During the lifetime he or she seems oblivious to normal fears. There is also a tendency toward experiencing spontaneous healing if the native is trained to understand these principles.

Venus Quintile Pluto — Goaded on by his or her intuition this native sets precedents for others to follow. He or she is quite sympathetic to vibrations around the immediate vicinity. There is a pleasure in dredging things up out of the depths whether this be buried treasure from the floor of the ocean or ideas from a long-hidden volume of books.

Quintiles of Mars:

Mars Quintile Ceres — Being diplomatic is one of the assets of having this natal combination of planets. This person tries to work within the existing circumstances without complaining. He or she dresses well at work and knows how to remain calm in front of children and co-workers. If trained he or she can put psychic abilities to work in healing and realignment techniques.

Mars Quintile Pallas Athena — Such a mathematical investigator may be interested in exploring the advanced fields of astronomy or astrological research. Regardless of where this native works he or she will use his imagination in carrying out all assigned projects.

Mars Quintile Juno — A determined individual this person can spend hours in silence if the circumstances call for it. Early in life he or she shows signs of good muscle control and the ability to direct attention away from self. This native will follow the mate faithfully through a varied career and many moves. Such a person overcomes hardships with a quiet smile.

Mars Quintile Vesta — In many cases people with this natal aspect were required to flee from religious persecution. Whether this simply meant leaving the family circle or actually moving from one country to another there were still the breaking of old ties and bonds. With this aspect there is the faith to begin anew where the atmosphere is more secure.

Mars Quintile Jupiter — Any good writer can bridge the gap between his or her own imagination and the reader's sense of reality. So it is with this native who extracts the kernal of truth from philosophical teachings. He or she instinctively knows what people need at the moment.

Mars Quintile Saturn — Even though injuries are sustained in fighting conformity or rigidity in any form this native picks himself or herself up and strives again. Unusual leadership capabilities are shown by having this combination of planets in the natal horoscope. Even if this trait does not manifest by the native becoming important there are always people who will follow him or her in local activities.

Mars Quintile Uranus — A person having this natal aspect can develop the raw material in group situations. There is the ability to build a working unit of people from whatever is presently available. This individual can use ritualism to enthuse people.

Mars Quintile Neptune — By analyzing the present problems this native intuitively understands how to bring about the best solution possible. He or she would be comfortable working in hospital or research situations. There are often prophetic dreams at one period of life.

Mars Quintile Pluto — Even having to live through trauma is worth this chance to ponder the real purpose of life. This native probes into the depths of the subconscious to find answers for perplexing questions. He or she knows from earliest childhood that the answers are within the self, not found by asking anyone else.

Quintiles of Jupiter:

Jupiter Quintile Ceres — Whether this person has biological children or not he or she is given opportunities to show the parental love and concern with which he has been so blessed. There is a inborn understanding of how to give tender loving care without spoiling the growing youngster. Such a trait is also helpful in dealing with animals.

Jupiter Quintile Pallas Athena — This brilliant mind can be used to its fullest as a high official of either government or church. With such special insight the native is often chosen to serve as a political advisor. In several cases investigated where this aspect was present in the natal horoscope the individual had been named for a great religious leader of the past.

Jupiter Quintile Juno — Inborn stage presence enhances any performance this native cares to give. When talent is developed through discipline and adherence to formal training this native can achieve success in his or her chosen field. He or she mixes in the best society in the particular environment.

Jupiter Quintile Vesta — This native gladly fulfills requests made of him and is known as a cheerful server. He or she falls back on personal hardships as a foundation for understanding the problems of others. This is a good natal aspect for a counselor.

Jupiter Quintile Saturn — When this combination of planetary energies is available in the natal horoscope the native can accept great responsibility by looking at the karmic purpose behind the task. This individual is very aware of the law of cause and effect which applies to all facets of life. He or she develops great effectiveness by using his or her intuition and natural perception. Although this native may not practice a particular form of orthodox religious ritual he has sustaining personal faith.

Jupiter Quintile Uranus — If hereditary talents are developed this native can help mold a culture through his or her writings and lectures. Regardless of the size of his classes or audiences this person explains his brillant philosophies in a crisp, sharp manner of speaking. This is one aspect of an achiever.

Jupiter Quintile Neptune — When in a lighter mood this native can be a good impersonator. He or she molds a role into its own characterization taking different parts of living entities and blending them into a believable whole. When this is carried too far the person stops knowing when he is real and when he is acting. As an entertainer this native calms peoples' fears and anxieties as he or she makes them laugh. Despite the levity there is a scientific mind which could just as easily be channeled into basic research.

Jupiter Quintile Pluto — Although persons with this natal aspect were active in all types of professional endeavors they all had one thing in common. This blend of energies leads to eventual success and acclaim for the native.

Quintiles of Saturn, Uranus, Neptune and Pluto:

Because the slow moving planets create major and minor aspects only during certain years or periods the Quintiles for Saturn, Uranus, Neptune and Pluto will be considered in their respective time frames. Persons born during various years react against the background of historical events as much as from the natal horoscope.

Saturn Quintile Uranus — Because of the personal and emotional impact of this 72-degree aspect it will be difficult to suggest what effects this angle between planets had on recorded history. Perhaps it is only by looking at the mature behavior of persons born during that generation that a clue to the historical meaning of such an aspect will be possible. With the separating aspect between Saturn and Uranus occurring in 1907 and 1908, 1950 and 1977 there would be expected to be added insight into changes in managerial procedures, acceptance of major scientific discoveries, and rebellion against any form of authority to name a few. Such things did manifest during both the beginning and the middle of the century as listed above.

As Saturn approached Uranus at the 72-degree angle, or Quintile, in 1933 and 1977 there were drastic changes in the stability of the world's economy. People were truly being called upon to rely on their natural talents and abilities. There was also a renewal of interest in psychic readings and studies.

Saturn Quintile Neptune — During the separating phase of this aspect which occurred in 1924, 1961 and 1997 during the Twentieth Century there were unveiled some of the mysteries surrounding current religious beliefs. New approaches in medicine were being considered during the earlier two periods which came to fruition years later. As these planets approached at 72 degrees distance in 1910, 1946 and 1980 people were freeing themselves from mass consciousness and beginning to have more individual opinions.

There emerged, in these diversified times, an appreciation of resourcefulness.

Saturn Quintile Pluto — Saturn separated from this outermost planet during the years 1920, 1954 and again in 1990 as the world was regaining some stability after armed conflicts. In the earlier periods there was a beginning awareness of the value to be gained by looking intuitively into the beliefs of other peoples and their respective cultures. After the World War I and after the Korean conflict East and West had a chance to meet and begin to blend. Saturn and Pluto were approaching each other in 1908, 1941 and 1975. One factor that was common to these eras was the comprehension that intelligence was not always measured by the degrees awarded to an individual. Out of necessity new methods of measuring ability were being generally accepted.

Uranus Quintile Neptune — The only time these outer planets were in Quintile aspect was during 1960 when they were approaching to later conjunction. Since persons born during that year are just now approaching maturity it would be difficult to even speculate about true delineations of this aspect.

Uranus Quintile Pluto — As with the preceding aspect these two planets were in Quintile only once this century, during the approaching aspect in 1938 and 1939 just prior to the outbreak of World War II.

Neptune Quintile Pluto — The two outermost planets did not meet in the Quintile aspect during the Twentieth Century.

15

Square Aspect

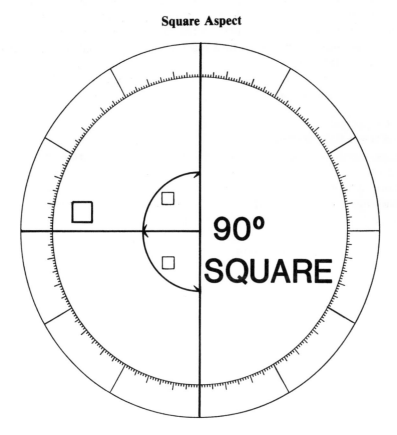

As when two roads cross each other at an intersection there must be a choice of which direction to proceed, the same 90-degree angle in Astrology forces decisions and activity. This action aspect has been written about more often than any other except perhaps the Conjunction. Contrary to past opinion about the Square creating bad luck or negative fortune for the native it simply forces the individual to react to situations at hand. Thus the Square may be considered as a stumbling block or a building block according to attitude of the observer.

Without Squares between planets in the natal horoscope there would be no fulfillment of the talents and benefits promised. These angles give the power and drive to accomplish, the energy and force to overcome inertia, the challenge and enterprise to pioneer, and the impulses to be creative.

In Uranian Astrology the Square, or 90-degree angle, is considered the basis of all action in the horoscope, the purpose around which the 90-degree dial and workboards were developed. Whether these angles are considered as obstacles in the path or stepping stones toward a goal they force constant activity between the planetary energies involved. Esoterically this may be considered the balancing of the four directions of Spirit, Soul, Body and Mind as the gravitational pulls from the four directions of Earth keep the planet spinning in space. With no Square aspects there would be a danger of inertia and laziness.

Because of the wealth of material about the Square aspect in other astrology textbooks only the following keywords will be considered here.

Glyph: □

Keywords of the Square:

achievement	confrontation	impulse	release
action	constriction	obstacle	stress
authoritative	crisis	originality	structure
challenge	discord	overcoming	struggle
choices	disorder	power	tumult
clashes	force	problems	work
conflict	frustration	reaction	worry

16

Tredecile Aspect

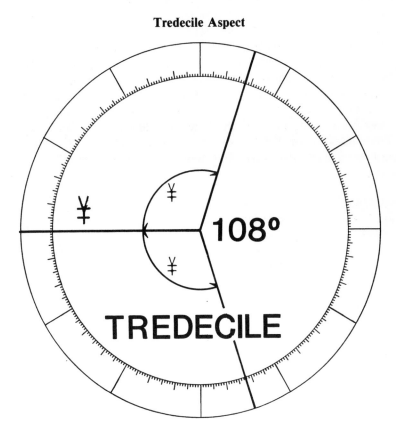

108°

TREDECILE

Though usually not considered as an aspect this 108-degree angle fits into the sequence of division of the 360-degree circle by the number ten, as part of the family of 36-72-108-144-180 which deals as much with esoteric matters as with exoteric events. The Tredecile tends to give a capacity for understanding the forces shaping cultural changes or the eventual destiny of mankind.

Strangely enough both the Roman Catholic nun with her rosary and the Buddhist monk with his mala beads are using the essence of this encircling quality as they finger the 108 beads in their respective chains. There are also 108 cannons in the Buddhist religious manuscripts.

This number 108 can be considered as a cosmic cycle of love that completes a turn of the spiral of life. Some Hermetic teachings suggest that it represents mastery of understanding the Logos.

When one planet approaches another planetary body at the Tredecile aspect there is an opening of the higher mind or an unfoldment of understanding or comprehension. As planets separate at 108 degrees they tend to lay cornerstones upon which more concrete materializations of the essences considered can be based. This later reaction can be likened to practical expression of an ethereal concept.

All aspects in this family or series show natural intuition whether it be developed to psychic abilities or used more as hunches. They tend to explain some of the inner workings of the mind which are not readily described by stronger action aspects. Unless a child is unusually perceptive these minor aspects show themselves more in later life than during the early years.

There is not sufficient research to present delineations for all the planets in Tredecile aspect to all others so these few keywords will be all that is contained in this particular book. An orb of 1 to 2 degrees is usually given for this aspect.

Glyph: ⅄

Keywords of the Tredecile:

aptitude	encircling	love	prophetic ability
base	imagination	mental stimulation	timing
cornerstone	insight	optimism	unfoldment

17

Trine Aspect

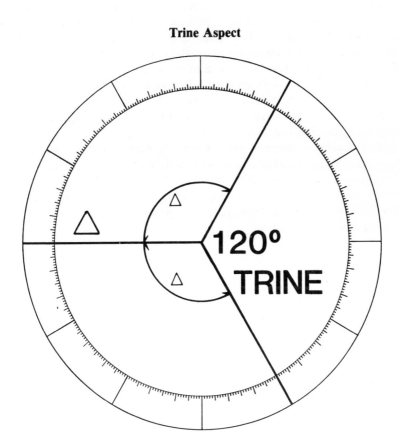

When the 360-degree circle is divided into three equal portions there is formed the 120-degree angle which is called the Trine aspect in Astrology. This particular triangle has been given many definitions over the centuries varying from extreme good luck to lack of ambition. Some schools of thought even deny use of this angle because it does not tend to indicate action or activity.

Even though the Trine is like the beautiful sailboat on a calm lake, sitting peacefully waiting for the wind to shift so that it can move, there are times in life when peace and gentleness are necessary amid the furor and tumult. A perfect horoscope would contain a balance of action and tranquil aspects so that the native could be both creative and calm.

The Trine aspect shows where help will appear in times of need, where creative ideas will suddenly flow through the mind, where the native can expect to find luck and good fortune, as well as where he or she may be lazy about using inherited talents. Most beneficial methods of recreation will be shown by the Trine aspects.

An ancient principle concerning the concept of the number Three states that whenever two persons, objects, businesses, organizations or any known things are brought together they immediately begin to form a third, but unseen, entity which is a combination of the two original beings or objects. This has proven quite true in the field of chemistry and physics where it can be demonstrated in a visible manner. Through analysis and counseling this esoteric truth has been found to be accurate also in relationships. So it may be with the Trine aspect where the potential for creativity is shown without being immediately manifested.

Where there are many Trines, especially Grand Trines, found in a horoscope the individual often needs the benefit of a Square, Opposition or other action aspect to use his or her natural abilities to the fullest.

Every basic text book in Astrology contains comments about the Trine aspect so the following keywords will complete the discussion of the 120-degree angle in this text.

Glyph: △
Keywords of the Trine:

absorbing	dramatizes	friendly	luck
benefits	easy	goodwill	optimism
blending	enthusiasm	harmony	overindulges
charisma	expansion	humor	recreation
comfort	expressive	increased value	reward
confidence	facilitate	joy	smooth
contact	fashionable	kindness	talents
creative	flow	lazy	understanding

18

Sesqui-Quadrate Aspect

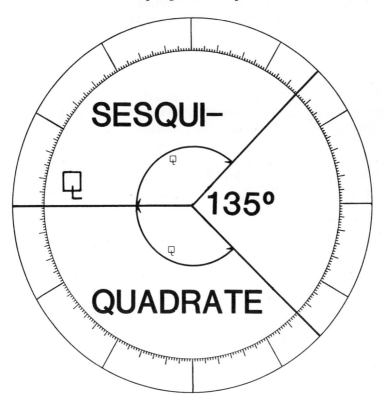

For astrologers pursuing techniques instigated by Alfred Witte and the Hamburg, Germany, School of Astrology 135 degrees holds equal importance with all other action angles. The Sesqui-Quadrate is formed when a circle or wheel is divided into eight equal portions thus making it the third angle in a series including the 45-degree Semi-Square and the 90-degree Square. Without a doubt this aspect does deal with activity and drive.

All action aspects denote exertion of the planetary energies involved. As the Sesqui-Quadrate occurs half way between an Opposition and a Square it is less likely to result in open conflict as to demand smoothing out of rough edges of the problem. Many times the 135-degree aspect is the last struggle before exposing an idea or concept to public scrutiny. The activity of a Sesqui-Quadrate often leads to clarification of an issue.

The snow-bound hermit who realizes that the only place to get life-sustaining water is under the frozen ice crust is faced with a dilemma. After this perception he or she takes the action of plunging his or her hand firmly through the clear solid. This creates an instant of shock and discomfort followed by the satisfaction that he now has the potential of a constructive solution to his immediate problem.

This same aspect is also termed Sesqui-Square and Tri-Oktil. Usually an orb of 2 to 3 degrees is used in natal horoscopes.

Glyph: ♬

Keywords of the Sesqui-Quadrate:

agitation	endurance	needs	release of tension
alterations	escapism	obstacles	remodeling
dangers	finishing up	plunges	rushes
deliberation	frustrating	potential	sensitive
difficulties	hurries	problems	selectivity
discord	intensity	propels	self criticism
disruptions	lack of control	rearrangement	urges
distinction	misuse	re-evaluate	willful

Sesqui-Quadrates of the Sun:

Sun Sesqui-Quadrate Moon — Lack of attentiveness causes this native to receive numerous scoldings. An innate poise and consideration overrules the friction created. Moping over problems only makes them more severe. From childhood to maturity whenever this person abuses power it is removed from his or her grasp. Frequent reprimands come from parents.

Sun Sesqui-Quadrate Mercury — This aspect is not possible in the natal horoscope because of the orbital patterns of Mercury around the Sun.

Sun Sesqui-Quadrate Venus — This aspect is not possible in the natal horoscope because of the orbital patterns of Venus around the Sun.

Sun Sesqui-Quadrate Mars — Slight miscalculations lead to major failures for persons having this aspect in their natal horoscopes. They must learn to work slowly and ploddingly toward objectives for the best results. In contests the lesson will be that learning good sportsmanship is as important as winning.

Sun Sesqui-Quadrate Ceres — Danger lurks behind simple confrontations for this person whose movements are constrained. He or she prefers a rural setting for the home. Extremely hard work over a prolonged period of time depletes the energy reserve. There is a tendency towards problems with diverticulitis. Being extremely concerned about nutrition stems from early allergies which can usually be controlled with diet.

Sun Sesqui-Quadrate Pallas Athena — Being dissatisfied with employment opportunities often comes about because of wrong attitude. The proper inner attitude determines possibility of success. Desire, anxiety and feelings of alienation block receptivity and turn other people away. To serve in any capacity demands a readiness to respond to others. This native needs to learn not to vacillate from doubt to confidence, from exuberance to fear, and from generosity to miserliness. He or she must look for the constructive solution for this frustration.

Sun Sesqui-Quadrate Juno — Curious costumes worn to parties, meetings and other public gatherings are just a method of getting attention. Dressing in such unorthodox fashion to defy convention is another way of crying out against being suppressed. This native finds it hard to fit into the confines of traditional marriage or any form of legal partnership yet fears being left alone. Within this contradictory framework he or she struggles to find the answer. An attempt to stifle creativity in others usually stems from personal jealousy.

Sun Sesqui-Quadrate Vesta — Action follows thought and it is important for this native to keep his or her intentions pure. Regardless of the importance of a belief or an activity he must not try to influence others beyond their ability to accept. When people are ready they will learn about certain factors or follow other roads, but not until the proper time. Rather than be caught up in unpleasant situations a person with this aspect would do well to listen to wise counsel before exerting influence.

Sun Sesqui-Quadrate Jupiter — Errors seem to multiply once they begin showing up for this native. Various problem solving techniques can be helpful to fall back on if they have been thoroughly ingrained through rigorous training. Desire for one more win lies behind many failures. If he or she would be willing to quit while on top it would help. Even the luckiest person eventually loses a toss of the dice.

Sun Sesqui-Quadrate Saturn — Services or benefits are regularly curtailed without a decrease in the cost so that this native usually feels slighted by not having his or her demands met as anticipated. Being a deliberate and determined person he or she has the wisdom to abandon a futile struggle before being completely defeated. There is the ever present threat of being tempted to manipulate others out of selfish motives for power.

Sun Sesqui-Quadrate Uranus — Nervous tension which is allowed to get out of hand leads to hypertension. This native acts impulsively unless there are other factors in the horoscope to equalize this tendency. During the lifetime his or her career demands rapid moves in unexpected directions. This aspect brings a great deal of excitement into the native's life.

Sun Sesqui-Quadrate Neptune — A person having this particular aspect finds it confusing about which side of his or her complex personality to display in public. This may even take the form of wearing clothing traditionally belonging to the opposite sex. Eventually he or she will learn that manipulating persons in positions of authority can backfire. Without relieving factors this aspect brings alternating periods of depression and exultation.

Sun Sesqui-Quadrate Pluto — Secrets will eventually be exposed to public view so it is important for this native to be wary of his or her private activities. Avoiding contact with even minor criminals is wise.

Sesqui-Quadrates of the Moon:

Moon Sesqui-Quadrate Mercury — With a certain amount of time alone to prevent tension buildup this individual will be a better student as a child and a more efficient adult worker. Lack of compromise in emergency situations can be disastrous. He or she has many disagreements with women. Writings are either too complex for others to understand or he or she may author a few obscure booklets. There is a need to give associates freedom to express their own ideas.

Moon Sesqui-Quadrate Venus — Strength is more often shown by remaining still and calm than by displays of temper and swirls of busyness. Because of this inability to persevere in the face of pressure the native suffers frequent setbacks to his or her personal ambitions. Excessive criticism only makes demands more impossible to carry out. It is important to look for the similarities not the differences between people in order to tame the emotions aroused by this aspect.

Moon Sesqui-Quadrate Mars — Resentment of rules lasting beyond adolescence shows emotional immaturity. When a person continually criticizes others it gets boring and people quit listening even to valid comments. Pride goes before a fall unless he or she learns the lesson of humility.

Moon Sesqui-Quadrate Ceres — In extreme cases this may be one of the factors in the horoscope showing infertility or denial of children for either male or female. More generally this aspect tends to make the native more aggressive; good at starting businesses and propelling others into action. Being brusque and harsh is often a cover up for sentimental emotions which he or she does not know how to express.

Moon Sesqui-Quadrate Pallas Athena — An old Chinese proverb says one should not marry a powerful maiden. It probably dealt with women having many hard or action aspects between the feminine planets. This native, whether male or female, is often too busy espousing crusades for equality to take much interest in his family or home life. Probably a more difficult aspect for a woman to handle than a man.

Moon Sesqui-Quadrate Juno — Arguing about trivialities only indicates that the native has hidden anxieties about his or her own importance. Striving for the wrong goals can be truly frustrating. There is need to contemplate about choices before they are made rather than complain after the accomplished fact. With this aspect it is important to learn to be forgiving of the mistakes of others.

Moon Sesqui-Quadrate Vesta — There is an early learning to suppress the emotions when this aspect is present in the natal horoscope. Eventually this wall must be broken down in order for the person to release resentment and fears. Before that occurs doubts will crop up which will keep this native from being as confident as he or she would like to be. In extreme cases this aspect shows lack of proper nourishment.

Moon Sesqui-Quadrate Jupiter — Unwarranted optimism leads to eventual disappointments. Although it is nice to be cheerful and positive there must be some substantiation behind even the simplest schemes in order for them to materialize. Moderation is the solution to a more stable life for this native. Being either completely dependant on someone else or being the total support of another weakens both persons involved. There is a need to learn when to quit a failing endeavor.

Moon Sesqui-Quadrate Saturn — Healthy skepticism is constructive especially when dealing with experimental situations. Throughout life experiences will occur to give this native the opportunity to learn to be more disciplined. Until this lesson is learned there is a tendency to leave tasks after a superficial attempt at completing them. Then persons in authority demand that deficiencies be remedied.

Moon Sesqui-Quadrate Uranus — It is hard for persons having this aspect in their horoscopes to express their inner emotions. They rebel at curtailment of their personal freedom. A gruff veneer hides fear of not being liked. He or she is often jealous without sufficient reason. There is an emotional disorientation any time these two planets are in a tension angle with each other.

Moon Sesqui-Quadrate Neptune — Expected sympathy is usually not forthcoming so this native is frequently disappointed. With frequent dreams and nightmares it is wise to learn to deal with them constructively. Keeping a dream journal, working with universal symbols and attending workshops aimed at analyzing these tools of the subconscous are some avenues. There may be multiple psychic experiences.

Moon Sesqui-Quadrate Pluto — Simple curiosity is not always understood by others and is often criticized as snooping. This is a good aspect for a newspaper reporter or persons involved in any form of investigative work. Even with proper protection it is wise to stay away from criminal elements. Foods that are slightly tainted or beginning to be spoiled can make this native ill.

Sesqui-Quadrates of Mercury:

Mercury Sesqui-Quadrate Venus — This aspect is not possible in the natal horoscope because of the orbital patterns of Venus.

Mercury Sesqui-Quadrate Mars — Taking calculated risks over the years makes some lucky people quite wealthy while leaving others destitute. So it is with natives having this natal astrological aspect which can be used as an advantage or a difficulty. He or she lets discussions which should be common conversations become heated arguments. Daily life would be much quieter by realizing more methodical people don't make snap judgments before the facts are all presented. But that style of conduct is calm and boring for thrill seekers.

Mercury Sesqui-Quadrate Ceres — Initiating new projects before family or occupational responsibilities are in hand creates more irritation than a brief delay of the fresh start. Somehow this particular combination of planets pushes the native into premature action. He or she must learn when it is time to keep still and when it is expedient to move. Rest and movement are not antithetical but in rhythm with natural cycles. Once into the confusion this native talks too much about the minute details of each task involved, to the extent of becoming a boring conversationalist. Authors find this aspect limits their writing vocabulary.

Mercury Sesqui-Quadrate Pallas Athena — Some minor speech difficulties such as childhood lisping are found with this aspect. Anger or frivolous jokes are equally out of place in serious situations as this native soon learns to his or her regret. This is a good aspect for such a controversial career as a talk show host who must be able to create a certain amount of controversy in order to keep his program interesting.

Mercury Sesqui-Quadrate Juno — Demanding that everything be equalized either by signing formal agreements or by taking constant tallies shows a dread of being cheated. A man or woman having this natal aspect worries about other people not being fair with him or her. If this attitude persists he becomes a cantankerous elder. Taken to the extreme this native may write a bizarre will rejecting friends and relatives whom he believes have slighted him.

Mercury Sesqui-Quadrate Vesta — General resignation about unpleasant episodes in life brings harmony and peace, so the lesson of submission is important for this native to learn. There is no way one person can persuade another to turn from his or her erroneous path. No matter what his good intentions each man saves only himself. Without relief elsewhere in the natal horoscope this aspect restricts communication and study.

Mercury Sesqui-Quadrate Jupiter — Moderation in making plans would keep this native from overspending both money and energy. He or she needs to learn to pare down to necessities in his or her schemes. It is essential to begin to reflect on the past, review previous actions, weigh the checks and balances, and meditate on expected goals, before taking any action. When in difficulty the way out is not through accepting bribes or loans which can lead to complex legal problems.

Mercury Sesqui-Quadrate Saturn — Quick retorts create long range problems. Being regimented into a mold is difficult with someone having this aspect in his or her natal horoscope. Sometimes being held down leads to despondency. Responsibility must be learned through experience. This person tries to use inadequate equipment or talents to achieve success, which leads to catastrophe.

Mercury Sesqui-Quadrate Uranus — Rebellious outbursts startle other people and sometimes do great harm. The person having such a natal aspect often enjoys sharing shocking news or gossip regardless of the long range effect it may have, showing an insensitivity to the feelings of friends and family. In extreme cases this aspect shows deviation from accepted sexual patterns. Whether man or woman the native is quite changeable in ideas and beliefs, following first one persuasion and then running after another guru.

Mercury Sesqui-Quadrate Neptune — Being disillusioned is no excuse for misrepresenting the truth to others. Since grieving over past events doesn't replace the loss there is no point in lying to draw associates into personal misery. This native needs to learn the difference between reality and imagination. However, use of this aspect by fiction writers can be constructively creative. Such natives as Hans Christian Anderson have penned delightful fairy tales out of this genius of fancy.

Mercury Sesqui-Quadrate Pluto — Even through fluctuating fortunes this native needs to remember that discretion is the better part of wisdom. Self confidence leads to poise and success, where insecurity comes out as blustering boasts which impress no one. Sarcastic or provocative comments make enemies not friends.

Sesqui-Quadrates of Venus:

Venus Sesqui-Quadrate Mars — Hard work is usually the path of this native from early childhood through later years. Sometimes this fills the gap left by romantic disappointments. He or she falls in and out of love quickly, often being premature in declaring his or her affections. Expensive gifts are given more out of personal insecurity than appreciation of the recipient.

Venus Sesqui-Quadrate Ceres — Wise investments of time and money are made by relating freely to both superiors and employees. Friendship is easier for this native to handle than romance. This man or woman can be overly indulgent with either people or pets whom he or she attracts. There is a need to balance the desire nature. Parents with this aspect are cautioned against smothering their children with too much concern.

Venus Sesqui-Quadrate Pallas Athena — If conditions and circumstances are not satisfactory it is easier to move into another situation than fight the status quo. This native takes on challenges at work and at home rather than compromise any principles. Such generosity of effort, especially on the part of co-workers, may only bring the individual disappointment. It is better to avoid involvement in partnerships where there is not some sharing of ideals. People often resent their benefactor rather than admit their own weaknesses.

Venus Sesqui-Quadrate Juno — That an emotionally structured relationship leads to frigidity both physically and emotionally should be borne in mind when this individual wonders at the lack of spontaneous affection given to him or her. Quite often the appetite is depressed in times of trauma or chaos.

Venus Sesqui-Quadrate Vesta — This native is inclined toward giving affection to help persons in time of sorrow or depression. However, he will just as easily deny tenderness to show rejection or disapproval. Often he or she leaves comfortable surroundings to pursue a purpose. Failure to achieve desired goals comes out of being restless and indecisive rather than firm and deliberate.

Venus Sesqui-Quadrate Jupiter — Helpfulness and charitable acts must be sincere to really aid others. Rather than try to be a martyr an individual having this natal aspect should be patient and discreet in offering assistance. It is important that all persons involved be able to keep their self respect and dignity to avoid resentment.

Venus Sesqui-Quadrate Saturn — Anxiety about security and health lead to periods of depression unless alleviated by other factors in the horoscope. Superiors often complain about minor offences in the work area. This may be as minor as parental disapproval shown about tardiness to finish household tasks to the foreman's rejection of a completed pulley system. Often there is volunteer service with elderly persons such as Meals on Wheels, the hospice movement or Grandparents Anonymous.

Venus Sesqui-Quadrate Uranus — Financial stability looks more inviting than the fluctuating income which this native finds himself facing because of his or her interest in unusual projects. Sometimes he or she finds it impossible to collect insurance or retirement payments due because of the death of a near relative. This individual is inflamed with desire to face the exciting and unknown even if it proves to be an illusion; a factor quite necessary in an innovative artist or research scientist.

Venus Sesqui-Quadrate Neptune — Results of overspending creep up slowly to sudden awareness of serious financial debt for a man or woman having this natal astrological aspect. Disruptive schedules and irregular employment create an uneven flow of money so that it is difficult to plan or budget in a sensible manner. This man or woman has rather vague responses to offers of affection.

Venus Sesqui-Quadrate Pluto — There is a tendency to be deceived by glamorous frosting rather than see the reality of a situation. Subtle undercurrents are lost on this native. Through use of meditation he or she can achieve altered states of consciousness though not always the wisdom to know how to handle this portion of discipleship.

Sesqui-Quadrates of Mars:

Mars Sesqui-Quadrate Ceres — Creative energy is blocked when fear, anger or suspicion is aroused. Any action aspect between these two planets tends to disrupt the energy flow. By letting the gentleness of Ceres remain an internal force while Mars initiative manifests externally this aspect can become a constructive force. The native should remember to eat properly and at regular intervals in order to nourish and revitalize the body. It is like a fighter keeping in training so that he can be prepared for the rigors of the actual bout.

Mars Sesqui-Quadrate Pallas Athena — The diligent worker often labors beyond his level of peak efficiency. Time out for periodic rest is necessary not an indulgence. There is a scattering of the energies with this aspect. High fevers are likely when this native is ill.

Mars Sesqui-Quadrate Juno — A self-centered attitude separates this individual from his loved ones. There is also a tendency to hold on long after the relationship has ended, whether concerning friendship or marriage. He or she may become quite angry at being disciplined or limited in any way.

Mars Sesqui-Quadrate Vesta — There is a burning desire to achieve when this aspect appears in the natal horoscope. Yet the timing is often not right for this native to accomplish his greatest potential. This extreme effort arouses distrust in others so they hinder rather than help him or her. There is more wisdom in waiting to be asked than in volunteering so quickly. This aspect shows a need for learning patience.

Mars Sesqui-Quadrate Jupiter — When this aspect is present in the natal horoscope the native is frustrated by having less authority than desired. He or she cannot express himself forcefully enough to make people respond. In some cases this anger is shown as religious bigotry and overconfidence while in others the individual acts overly cautious, almost timid. Another possibility is prudishness which covers the individual's own sensuality.

Mars Sesqui-Quadrate Saturn — Some highly emotional people work at unusual professions in their attempt to rebel at society. When Mars and Saturn are thrown together in hard or action aspects there is usually a struggle against being made to fit into a mold. This manifests as criticism of all authority figures.

Mars Sesqui-Quadrate Uranus — Brillant minds driven by ideas may be denied credit for their great achievements during the lifetime. Co-workers of these people often meet with sudden accidents. A native with this aspect can be quite dangerous when aroused by anger or unusually inventive when inspired. Sudden brainstorms make him or her uncomfortable to live around.

Mars Sesqui-Quadrate Neptune — It is hard for this native to keep secrets from becoming public knowledge. He or she is magnetically drawn to ideas and loves to research a good mystery whether it be in fiction or real life. In some cases it is better for persons having this aspect to shy away from occult study or investigation. It is an aspect which energizes the desire to dig for the truth through long and tedious research.

Mars Sesqui-Quadrate Pluto — This combination of energies makes it possible for the native to be willing to face public censure to work out his or her own ideas. There may even be breaks with the family over personal beliefs or ideals. Sometimes there is the impulsive reaction, almost to the point of frenzy, caused by spasmodic adrenal secretions.

Sesqui-Quadrates of Jupiter:

Jupiter Sesqui-Quadrate Ceres — There is a time for rest and a time for activity which this native needs to learn. Fruitless actions are more useless than keeping still in some instances. This native has the tendency to over-react or overwork to stress. This aspect leads one to do such things as plant a dozen tomato seedlings in the space for three or four.

Jupiter Sesqui-Quadrate Pallas Athena — Too many responsibilities to handle easily can lead to failure on all sides. This native has trouble keeping a job because he or she tends to anticipate more than the occupation will reward. His or her reaction is to be constantly whining or complaining about working conditions when reality falls short of the ideal. There can also be trouble with unemployment insurance.

Jupiter Sesqui-Quadrate Juno — Eventually the native having this aspect will develop a clear view of his or her spouse having little to do with the romantic notions of early marriage. With perspective gained through patience and endurance of unpleasant situations there can be real fulfill-ment in a relationship. This aspect deals with rounding off the sharp corners in a partnership. It may be temporarily grating, like the sound of filing fingernails, but the final result is as smooth and appealing as the finished manicure.

Jupiter Sesqui-Quadrate Vesta — Intensity of purpose is fine but the moderate approach achieves more in the long run. This native needs to examine his or her lack of control or direction in order to be more effective. There is a tendency here to escape into religious or philanthropic activities when there are personal problems.

Jupiter Sesqui-Quadrate Saturn — Disappointments crop up because of improper planning and incomplete training of both self and others for this native. There is a need for him or her to pick up the slack. It is like the yarn or thread which becomes snarled from sewing with too long a strand. The lesson here is to accept responsibility for fewer tasks and complete them before going on to new jobs.

Jupiter Sesqui-Quadrate Uranus — Working with unique electrical equip-ment is a joy as well as a problem for persons having this natal aspect. He or she will be enthused about ideas far beyond the present understanding of most people. Several great inventors having this aspect had to undergo much stress and difficulty to achieve their goals. On the negative side, this aspect can lead to the native desiring a "thrill a minute" kind of existence.

Jupiter Sesqui-Quadrate Neptune — With this aspect the native would do well to beware of unseen details in all situations. Much theoretical research may be begun by this person which will not reach fruition. Also, there is the danger of being deceived by an impersonator or of being tempted to impersonate another for devious reasons.

Jupiter Sesqui-Quadrate Pluto — Nothing delights this native as much as to arouse adverse public response to an idea or theory. Sometimes there is a love-hate relationship which exists during much of the lifetime. Very strong emotions are best put to constructive use if this native wishes to have any emotional peace and satisfaction.

Sesqui-Quadrates of Saturn, Uranus, Neptune and Pluto:

Because the slower moving planets create major and minor aspects only during certain years or periods the Sesqui-Quadrates for Saturn, Uranus, Neptune and Pluto will be considered in their respective time frames. Persons born during various years react against the background of historical events.

Saturn Sesqui-Quadrate Uranus — Rumblings or problems were heard all over the world during the two separating Sesqui-Quadrate aspects between these two diverse planets during this century. Social activists were writing about their favorite causes, conservative leaders were defeated and overcome by more liberal chieftains, scientifically oriented people were born who would eventually change the world of commerce and communication. During the 1913 through 1915 period the early Bolshevik uprisings in Russia mirrored a struggle against leadership which became world wide. During the late years of the 1950's science and industry were vying for power in a world being made ready for the scientific geniuses born into it. This was also the period of the first true hyperkenetic children being born.

During the approaching Sesqui-Quadrate aspects between Saturn and Uranus in the Twentieth Century there were false economy upswings which led to later serious recessions. It was during this period of 1924 to 1925 that some of the most innovative minds of the century were born. Therefore, it will be interesting to see how the leaders born in the early 1970's behave at their maturity.

Saturn Sesqui-Quadrate Neptune — This aspect seems to behave more as a dissolving of long upheld barriers than any other single factor. During the periods when Saturn was approaching Neptune during 1904 to 1906, the early 1940's, and 1973 to 1975 there were many sudden advances in methods of communication. As the railroads moved westward around the turn of the century the telephone and telegraph spread throughout the country to link Americans from coast to coast as never before. Television rapidly became a fixture in most American homes during the early 1940's and movies showed rapidly developed news films of the war on both fronts. By the mid 1970's communications satellites were sending signals of far flung events into suburban homes within hours of their happening. Some metaphysical leaders have stated that 1974 was a year when great esoteric truths first became available to the masses. Perhaps during the 2008 approaching Sesqui-Quadrate between Saturn and Neptune such physical barriers as the Great Wall of China may tumble and mental barriers to the study of parapsychology may vanish.

When Saturn separates from Neptune at 135 degrees away there seems to be a general unrest which eventually expands the areas it affects. Labor unrest beset management of major industries all over the world at the 1931 and 1967 time periods. During this same period there was also an expansion of the field of aeronautics. The first air-passenger services were developed in the 1930's to supplement the early mail flights. During the middle of the 1960's there was a decided concentration in aero-space research and development as well as many manned flights. Perhaps by the separating Sesqui-Quadrate in 2001 there will be space travel for the multitudes.

Saturn Sesqui-Quadrate Pluto — Missionaries returned to this country from the Middle East telling of the atrocities of the Chinese throughout the Boxer Rebellion during the early Saturn-Pluto Sesqui-Quadrate at the turn of the century. Other approaching phases of this aspect occurred in the mid 1930's when gangsters ran rampant in major American cities and in the late 1960's during the effective, but unorganized, youth rebellion in this country. All three of these time periods brought heartbreak as well as change to the traditions and morals of the population.

When Saturn is separating from a Sesqui-Quadrate with Pluto there seems to be a fascination with glamour and charisma. There was the Flapper Era during the late 1920's which kept people from facing economic problems slightly veiled by a changing economy. During the early 1960's the Kennedy election brought in a new era of glamour on the American political scene. Appearances became more important than credentials in obtaining promotion or power. The Ivy League look and popular physical fitness programs altered the reassuring image of the staid business man. The need to analyze one's personal worth was popular during both of these time periods. When Saturn and Pluto are next in this configuration during the late 1990's there may again be a need to examine the lack of control or direction of large groups of people.

Uranus Sesqui-Quadrate Neptune — The only time period affected by this aspect during the current century was when Uranus and Neptune were fluctuating in and out of aspect during 1931 through 1934. From people born in these years came the armies who fought in the Korean conflict and began to rebel against the concept of political wars. These were the children born during the middle of the depression years when luxuries were few and necessities were hard to obtain. There is little wonder that adults born with this aspect find security in material possessions which were so lacking during their childhood.

Uranus Sesqui-Quadrate Pluto — The single time when this aspect was active during the Nineteen Hundreds was during World War I which disrupted the patterns and lives of an entire universe. This approaching aspect lasted from 1915 through 1918 and brought all the difficulties, dangers and agitation expected from reaction between such powerful planets of change and upheaval.

Neptune Sesqui-Quadrate Pluto — No such aspect occurred between these two planets during the Twentieth Century.

19

Biquintile Aspect

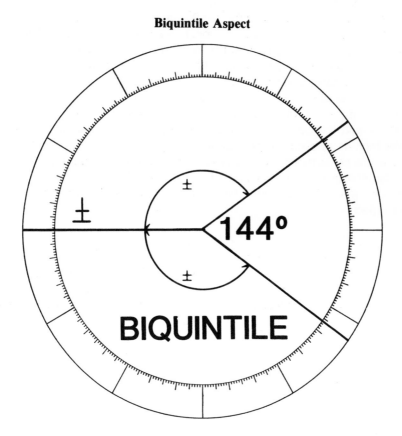

Esoteric significance is given to all the aspects derived by dividing the circle into five equal portions. Partly this has evolved from the ancient concept of the number Five representing the spiritual value of man. Another meaning of five deals with senses of smell, touch, feeling, hearing and sight. A Biquintile aspect is the second of the series formed by cutting the wheel into five pieces. This is called a multiple of the Quintile, or 72-degree aspect. Thus many of the interpretations are similar.

Dr. Elisabeth V. Bacon of Columbus, Ohio, considers the 144 degree Biquintile aspect to be one significator of a Major Adept who has conquered earthly temptations through strict discipline. This can occur in past lives or in the present incarnation. She further states that the Biquintile indicates leadership qualities for an individual who uses his mental abilities constructively.

Horoscopes of several renown authors and speakers show that the Biquintile signifies an understanding of the subtle forces behind current social movements. These people are capable of phrasing brillant ideas so they can be accepted for popular publication.

In addition to being resourceful, the Biquintile acts much more like colorful garnishes on a party platter. Though it is not the main ingredient or aspect this minor angle adds a skillful touch to enhance the pleasure of the diners. By such intrinsic properties the Biquintile serves as the catalyst to augment the native's analytical abilities.

This aspect shows the child who has the aptitude to amuse himself for long periods of time or the adult who derives pleasure from his or her own pursuits and hobbies without help from others. The Biquintile indicates great reserves of power or perception.

There is not sufficient research to present delineations for all the planets in Biquintile aspect to all others so these few keywords will be all that is contained in this particular book. An orb of 1 to 2 degrees is usually given for this aspect.

Glyph: ±
Keywords of the Biquintile:

adeptship	creative	improves	regeneration
advantages	garnishes	penetrates	resourceful
clairvoyance	great reserve	perception	self expression
constructive	helps	pleases	unnoticed

20

Quincunx Aspect

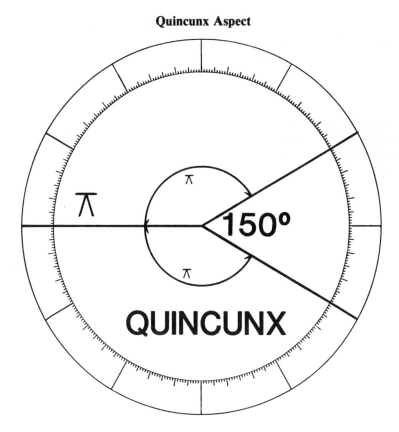

The Quincunx aspect, comprising 150 degrees of a circle, is one geometric figure which must be modified or revised because it cannot stand alone. Because of the very nature of the configuration this energy topples either to one side or the other. One of the two planets involved will be under constant strain until views are changed concerning the planetary energies involved.

When there is no stability there is a constant need to perfect techniques and procedures within the areas involved. Demands seem to arise simultaneously so there is constant need to pay attention to small details or suffer the consequences of hasty actions.

The Quincunx aspect is also commonly called the Inconjunct and has been written about widely in the last five years. Many astrologers now consider it a major aspect, particularly in health affairs. Both Francis Sakoian and Robert Pelletier have included many delineations for planets in Quincunx aspects in their books so you are referred to these and other texts for particular planetary influences with the 150 degree relationship.

Upon occasion planets having 150 degrees between also form a Yod or "finger of God" relationship with yet a third planet. This occurs when two planets, both Quincunx the same third planet, are in sextile aspect to each other. In these cases all three planets involved must be considered together in delineation and prediction.

Glyph: ⊼
Keywords of the Quincunx:

analysis	demands	imposition	revision
adjustment	degenerate	malfunction	scrutinize
choice	dilemma	maturing process	selectivity
clarification	examine	modify	topples
decisions	exchange	reorientation	transition

21

Opposition Aspect

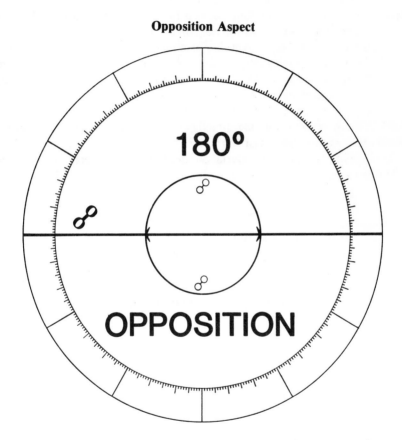

180°

OPPOSITION

Usually an object remains stagnant, or balanced, in nature so long as another object or energy does not touch or energize it. The same is true of people. Thus, we need the activation of the Opposition, or 180-degree aspect, to create confrontations which lead eventually to greater awareness. A pushing and pulling of opposing interests creates an understanding of both positions, but difficulty in finding an immediate solution to the problem presented. Long term solutions usually demand compromise and adjustments on both sides.

There is no such thing as being exactly equal in partnerships, marriages, or any other form of relationship. One person or group may need to go 60 percent of the way and the other need to move only 40 percent in order for balance to be achieved. As in the see-saw on a children's playground, the weight of two individuals using the equipment determines the fulcrum, or balance, point. In addition the original evenness of the wooden plank being used may vary from side to side even when two children of equal body weight are using the see-saw.

This same principle applies to planets found in Opposition in the natal horoscope. One native may find that in a Jupiter-Saturn Opposition he feels more comfortable relating to the Saturnian part of his nature rather than the Jupiter expansiveness. Another person may use the reverse pattern determined by the aspects from other planets to these two bodies, placement in the natal horoscope and general characteristics of the person. It is only through trial and error that a thorough understanding of the creative potential of this aspect can be realized. Neither planet can be ignored, but must be used in harmony with the one directly opposite it in the natal horoscope. Then there will be balance or harmony.

Because of the wealth of material on the Opposition aspect to be found in other astrology texts only the following keywords will be considered in this book.

Glyph: ☍

Keywords of the Opposition:

awareness	consummation	fusion	repolarizations
balance	cooperation	joining	separation
challenge	encounter	links	sharing
companionship	fertility	marriage	stretching
completion	fraternity	polarization	struggle
conflict	fruitful	push/pull	understanding
confrontation	fulfillment	reactions	union

Appendix A

NATAL HOROSCOPE CALCULATIONS

Name _____   Address _____

Birthdate _____   _____

Local Time _____ GMT _____   Tel: (Res) _____

Place _____   (Bus) _____

Lat/Long _____

		House Cusps		
S.T. (Noon) (Midn't) Prior to Birth . . . _____				
Time Elapsed to GMT Birth . . . . + _____		MC		
Acceleration of Mean Sun . . . . + _____		11		
Sum . . . . _____		12		
Long Corr (− if West, + if East) . . . . _____		ASC		
Sidereal Time of Birth . . . . + _____		2		
		3		

	NATAL	DECL	PROG 19___	DECL	NOTES
☉					
☽					
☿					
♀					
♂					
♃					
♄					
♅					
♆					
♇					
☊					
☋					
⚷					
⚸					
⚹					
⚴					

SOL ARC 19_____
PROG MC . . . . .
PROG ASC . . . .
DIR ASC . . . . . .
EQ (☉ / ☽) . . . .
VERTEX . . . . . .

MOON ECLIPSE BEFORE BIRTH

SUN ECLIPSE BEFORE BIRTH

FULL/NEW MOON BEFORE BIRTH

FULL/NEW MOON AFTER BIRTH

	FIRE	EARTH	AIR	WATER
CAR				
FIX				
MUT				

Appendix B

Table IV. Degree Conversion Table

Degrees	Aries	Taurus	Gemini	Cancer	Leo	Virgo	Libra	Scorpio	Sag	Cap	Aquarius	Pisces
1	1	31	61	91	121	151	181	211	241	271	301	331
2	2	32	62	92	122	152	182	212	242	272	302	332
3	3	33	63	93	123	153	183	213	243	273	303	333
4	4	34	64	94	124	154	184	214	244	274	304	334
5	5	35	65	95	125	155	185	215	245	275	305	335
6	6	36	66	96	126	156	186	216	246	276	306	336
7	7	37	67	97	127	157	187	217	247	277	307	337
8	8	38	68	98	128	158	188	218	248	278	308	338
9	9	39	69	99	129	159	189	219	249	279	309	339
10	10	40	70	100	130	160	190	220	250	280	310	340
11	11	41	71	101	131	161	191	221	251	281	311	341
12	12	42	72	102	132	162	192	222	252	282	312	342
13	13	43	73	103	133	163	193	223	253	283	313	343
14	14	44	74	104	134	164	194	224	254	284	314	344
15	15	45	75	105	135	165	195	225	255	285	315	345
16	16	46	76	106	136	166	196	226	256	286	316	346
17	17	47	77	107	137	167	197	227	257	287	317	347
18	18	48	78	108	138	168	198	228	258	288	318	348
19	19	49	79	109	139	169	199	229	259	289	319	349
20	20	50	80	110	140	170	200	230	260	290	320	350
21	21	51	81	111	141	171	201	231	261	291	321	351
22	22	52	82	112	142	172	202	232	262	292	322	352
23	23	53	83	113	143	173	203	233	263	293	323	353
24	24	54	84	114	144	174	204	234	264	294	324	354
25	25	55	85	115	145	175	205	235	265	295	325	355
26	26	56	86	116	146	176	206	236	266	296	326	356
27	27	57	87	117	147	177	207	237	267	297	327	357
28	28	58	88	118	148	178	208	238	268	298	328	358
29	29	59	89	119	149	179	209	239	269	299	329	359
30	30	60	90	120	150	180	210	240	270	300	330	360

Aspect Keyword List

Aspects are the verbs of Astrology. They tell what is happening between two or more planets in the chart or describe the action. Even if there were no signs or houses, aspects between planets would still exist because aspects merely measure the angular distance between planets or bodies in space. In the same vein, this text may be used by both Tropical and Sidereal astrologers for there is no mention of either houses or signs.

Glyph	Aspect	Degrees	Waxing Keyword	Degree	Waning Keyword
☌	Conjunction	0	Unity-Cycle	360	New Beginnings
⊥	Vigintile	18	Launching	342	Culmination
⅄	Semi-Octile	22½	Action	337½	Activity
√	Quindecile	24	Momentum	336	Braking
Y	Semi-Sextile	30	Emergence	330	Integration
⊥	Decile	36	Resources	324	Support
~	Novile	40	Gestation	320	Nurturing
∠	Semi-Square	45	Upsets	315	Stress
✿	Septile	51⅓	Focusing	308⅔	Commitment/Sacrifice
✳	Sextile	60	Opportunity	300	Application
Q	Quintile	72	Insight	288	Natural Abilities
☐	Square	90	Major Crisis	270	Test
✿B	Biseptile	102⅔	Zeal	257⅓	Dedication
¥	Tredecile	108	Cornerstone	252	Unfoldment
△	Trine	120	Expansion	240	Blending/Absorb
Q	Sesqui-Quadrate	135	Difficulties	225	Agitation
±	Biquintile	144	Advantage	216	Perception
⊼	Quincunx	150	Dilemma	210	Revision
✿T	Triseptile	154⅔	Consideration	205⅓	Cooperation
☍	Opposition	180	Re-evaluation	180	Repolarization

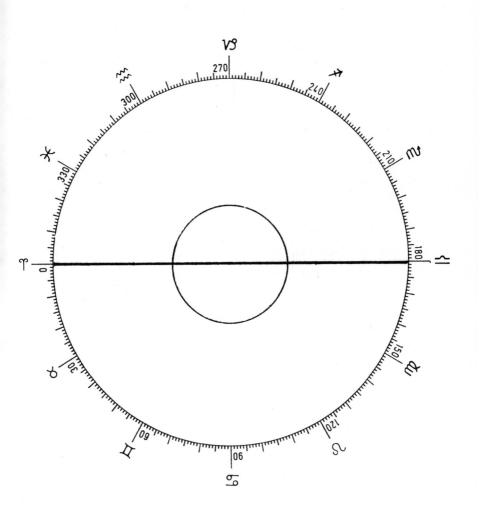

360 Degree Wheel
Figure 4

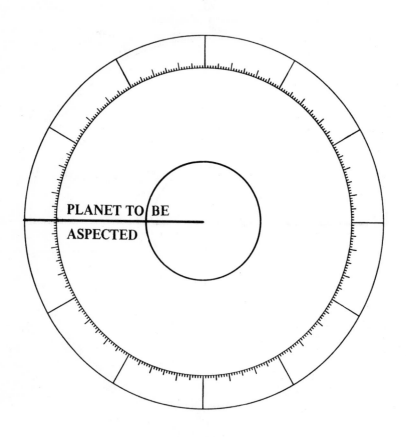

Aspect Wheel Example
Figure 5

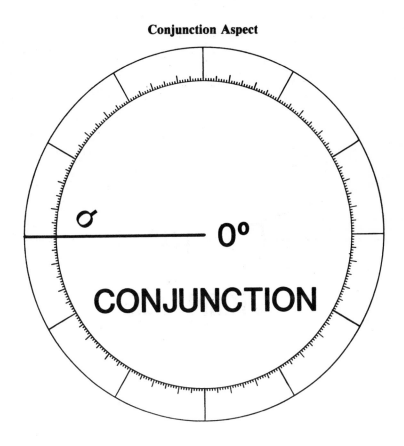

Conjunction Aspect

Conjunction Aspect Wheel
Figure 6

Cut out the above wheel. Place the arrow on the planet you wish to aspect. If there is another planet next to the arrow then you have a conjunction. If not, your planet does not have a conjunction aspect.

Vigintile Aspect

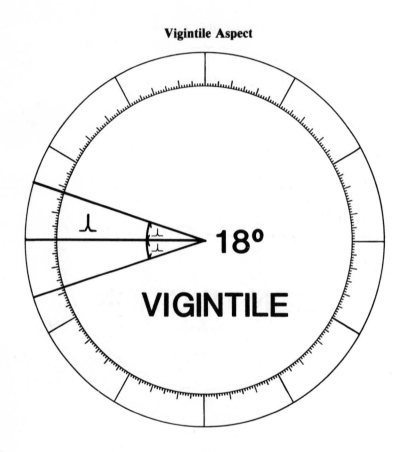

Vigintile Aspect Wheel
Figure 7

Cut out the above wheel. Place the arrow on the planet you with to aspect. If there is a planet at the end of either of the other lines you have a vigintile aspect. If not, your planet does not have a vigintile aspect.

Semi-Octile Aspect

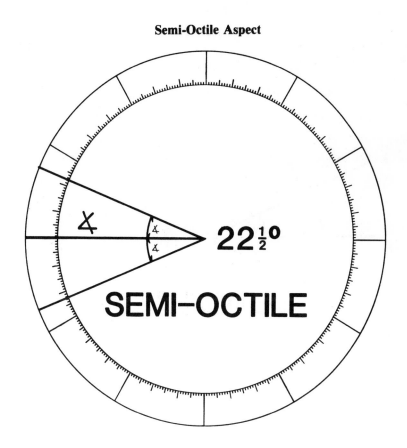

Semi-Octile Aspect Wheel
Figure 8

Cut out the above wheel. Place the arrow on the planet you wish to aspect. If there is a planet at the end of either of the other lines you have a semi-octile aspect. If not, your planet does not have a semi-octile aspect.

133

Quindecile Aspect

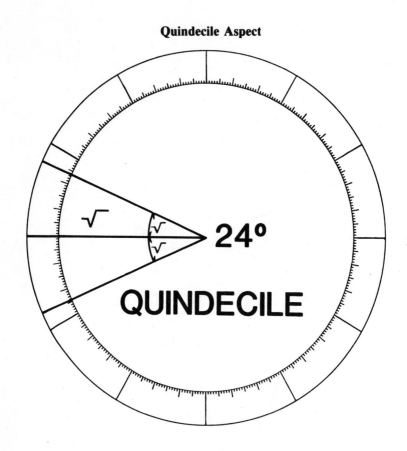

Quindecile Aspect Wheel
Figure 9

Cut out the above wheel. Place the arrow on the planet you wish to aspect. If there is a planet at the end of either of the other lines you have a quindecile aspect. If not, your planet does not have a quindecile aspect.

Semi-Sextile Aspect

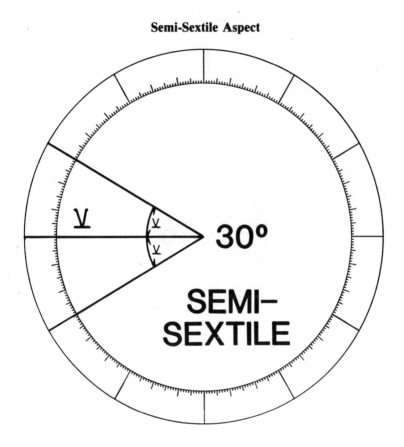

Semi-Sextile Aspect Wheel
Figure 10

Cut out the above wheel. Place the arrow on the planet you wish to aspect. If there is a planet at the end of either of the other lines you have a semi-sextile aspect. If not, your planet does not have a semi-sextile aspect.

Decile Aspect

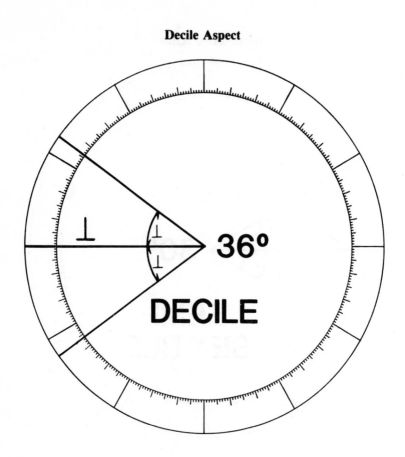

Decile Aspect Wheel
Figure 11

Cut out the above wheel. Place the arrow on the planet you wish to aspect. If there is a planet at the end of either of the other lines you have a decile aspect. If not, your planet does not have a decile aspect.

Novile Aspect

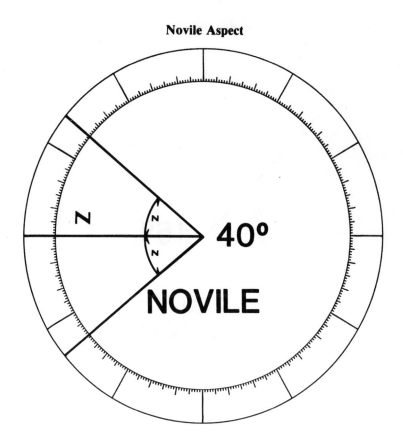

Novile Aspect Wheel
Figure 12

Cut out the above wheel. Place the arrow of the planet you wish to aspect. If there is a planet at the end of either of the other lines you have a novile aspect. If not, your planet does not have a novile aspect.

Semi-Square Aspect

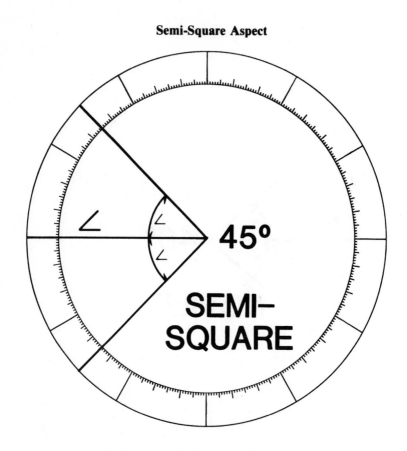

Semi-Square Aspect Wheel
Figure 13

Cut out the above wheel. Place the arrow on the planet you wish to aspect. If there is a planet at the end of either of the other lines you have a semi-square aspect. If not, your planet does not have a semi-square aspect.

Septile Aspect

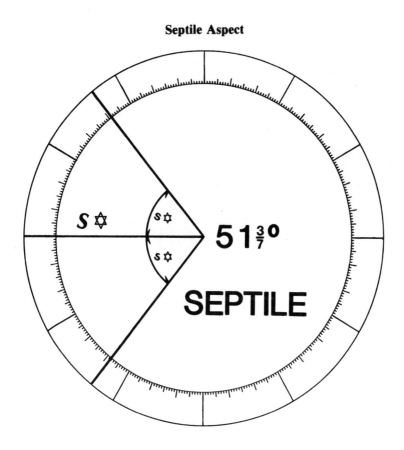

Septile Aspect Wheel
Figure 14

Cut out the above wheel. Place the arrow on the planet you wish to aspect. If there is a planet at the end of either of the other lines you have a septile aspect. If not, your planet does not have a septile aspect.

Sextile Aspect

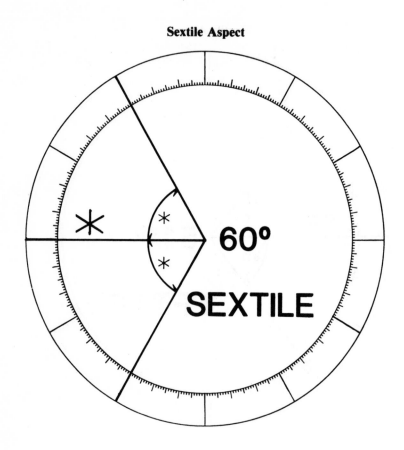

Sextile Aspect Wheel
Figure 15

Cut out the above wheel. Place the arrow on the planet you wish to aspect. If there is a planet at the end of either of the other lines you have a sextile aspect. If not, your planet does not have a sextile aspect.

Quintile Aspect

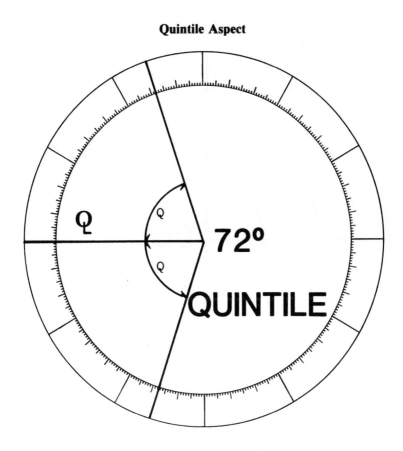

Quintile Aspect Wheel
Figure 16

Cut out the above wheel. Place the arrow on the planet you wish to aspect. If there is a planet at the end of either of the other lines you have a quintile aspect. If not, your planet does not have a quintile aspect.

Square Aspect

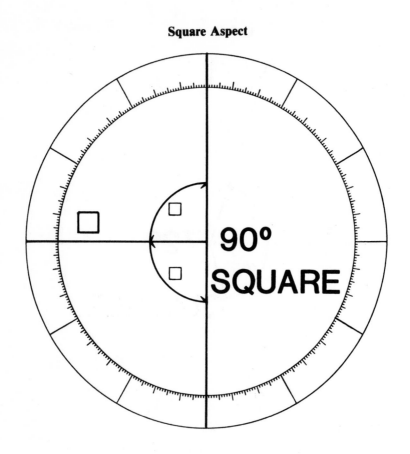

Square Aspect Wheel
Figure 17

Cut out the above wheel. Place the arrow on the planet you wish to aspect. If there is a planet at the end of either of the other lines you have a square aspect. If not, your planet does not have a square aspect.

Tredecile Aspect

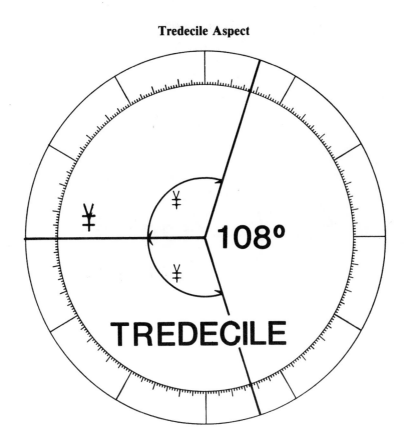

Tredecile Aspect Wheel
Figure 18

Cut out the above wheel. Place the arrow on the planet you wish to aspect. If there is a planet at the end of either of the other lines you have a tredecile aspect. If not, your planet does not have a tredecile aspect.

Trine Aspect

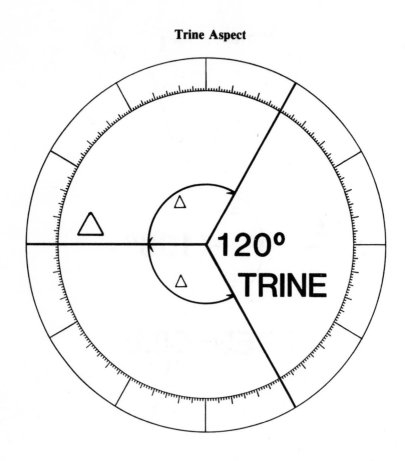

Trine Aspect Wheel
Figure 19

Cut out the above wheel. Place the arrow on the planet you wish to aspect. If there is a planet at the end of either of the other lines you have a trine aspect. If not, your planet does not have a trine aspect.

Sesqui-Quadrate Aspect

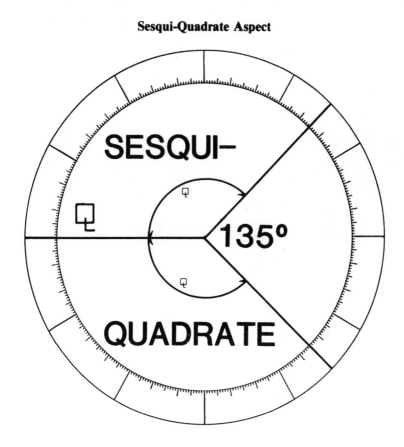

Sesqui-Quadrate Aspect Wheel
Figure 20

Cut out the above wheel. Place the arrow on the planet you wish to aspect. If there is a planet at the end of either of the other lines you have a sesqui-quadrate aspect. If not, your planet does not have a sesqui-quadrate aspect.

Biquintile Aspect

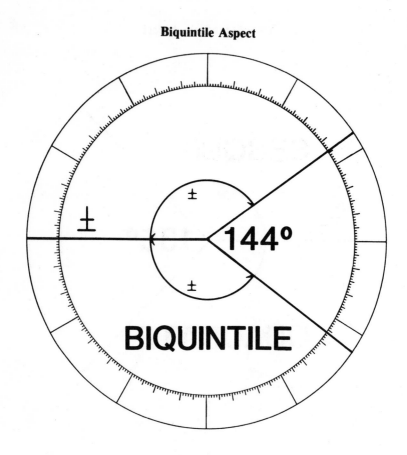

Biquintile Aspect Wheel
Figure 21

Cut out the above wheel. Place the arrow on the planet you wish to aspect. If there is a planet at the end of either of the other lines you have a biquintile aspect. If not, your planet does not have a biquintile aspect.

Quincunx Aspect

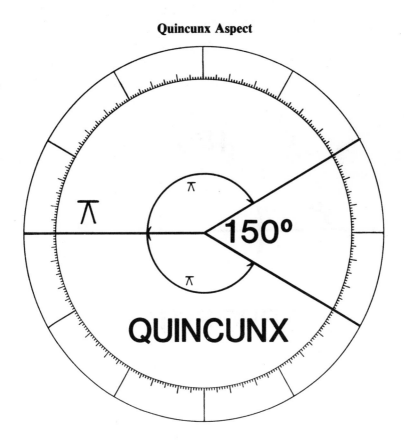

Quincunx Aspect Wheel
Figure 22

Cut out the above wheel. Place the arrow on the planet you wish to aspect. If there is a planet at the end of either of the other lines you have a quincunx. If not, your planet does not have a quincunx aspect.

Opposition Aspect

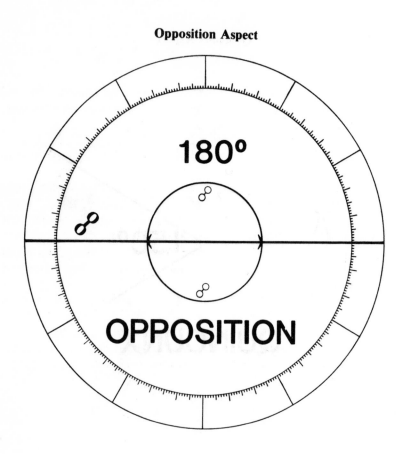

Opposition Aspect Wheel
Figure 23

Cut out the above wheel. Place the arrow on the planet you wish to aspect. If there is a planet at the end of the other line then you have an opposition aspect. If not, your planet does not have an opposition aspect.

Bibliography

Hawkins, John Robert, Transpluto or Should We Call Him Bacchus the Ruler of Taurus?, Dallas, Texas, Hawkins Enterprising Publications, 1978

Holt, Lee Wayne, The Astrological Thesaurus, Lee Wayne Holt, 1978

Koparker, Dr. Mohan, Aspects Magnified, Rochester, New York, Mohan Enterprises, 1978

Lofthus, Myrna, A Spiritual Approach to Astrology, Vantage Press, 1980

Meyer, Michael R., The Astrology of Relationship, Anchor Books, 1976

Rael, Leyla and Rudhyar, Dane, Astrological Aspects, New York, ASI Publishers, 1980

Sakoian, Frances and Acker, Louis, Major and Minor Approaching and Separating Aspects, Tempe, Arizona, American Federation of Astrologers, Inc., 1974

Sakoian, Frances and Acker, Louis, The Minor Aspects, F. Sakoian, 1978

Whitman, E.W., Aspects and Their Meanings, London, England, L.M. Fowler & Co., Ltd., 1970

Donath, Emma Belle, "Astrology Answers Passages," Stellium Quarterly, vols. 4:1 and 4:2, June, 1978 and September, 1978